THE ULTIMATE
WEST HAM UNITED FC
TRIVIA BOOK

A Collection of Amazing Trivia Quizzes
and Fun Facts for Die-Hard Hammers Fans!

Ray Walker

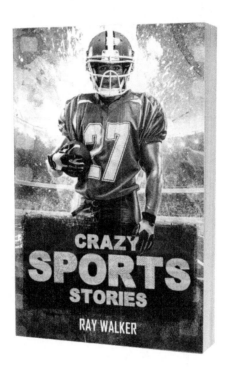

CONTENTS

Introduction..1

Chapter 1: Origins & History 3

    Quiz Time! 3

    Quiz Answers 8

    Did You Know? 9

Chapter 2: The Captain Class 12

    Quiz Time! 12

    Quiz Answers 17

    Did You Know? 18

Chapter 3: Amazing Managers...................................23

    Quiz Time! 23

    Quiz Answers 28

    Did You Know? 29

Chapter 4: Goaltending Greats 33

    Quiz Time! 33

    Quiz Answers 38

    Did You Know? 39

Chapter 5: Daring Defenders **43**

Quiz Time! 43

Quiz Answers.. 48

Did You Know?... 49

Chapter 6: Maestros of the Midfield **54**

Quiz Time! 54

Quiz Answers.. 59

Did You Know?.. **60**

Chapter 7: Sensational Strikers/Forwards **65**

Quiz Time! 65

Quiz Answers.. 70

Did You Know?... 71

Chapter 8: Notable Transfers/Signings **76**

Quiz Time! 76

Quiz Answers.. 81

Did You Know?... 82

Chapter 9: Odds & Ends... **86**

Quiz Time! 86

Quiz Answers.. 91

Did You Know?... 92

Chapter 10: Domestic Competition **95**

Quiz Time! 95

Quiz Answers.. 100

Did You Know? 101

Chapter 11: Europe and Beyond **104**

Quiz Time! 104

Quiz Answers 109

Did You Know? 110

Chapter 12: Top Scorers **115**

Quiz Time! 115

Quiz Answers 120

Did You Know? 121

Conclusion **125**

INTRODUCTION

After being formed as a factory soccer team in 1895, the Thames Ironworks and Shipbuilding Company FC evolved into West Ham United, one of England's most famous and beloved clubs. The East London side, commonly known as the Hammers, has been entertaining fans for well over a century with numerous pieces of silverware to show for its efforts.

The club has achieved success in its homeland as well as Europe, but as of 2021, a top-tier league championship had still eluded it. It hasn't been for lack of effort, though, as Hammers' players are well-known worldwide for their persevering attitude both on and off the pitch.

West Ham fans have plenty to be proud of from throughout the club's history, such as beating mighty Manchester United for the FA Cup while playing in the Second Division, but there have also been some disappointments along the journey.

It appears there are plenty more good times to come, though, as the 2020-21 side was one of the most competitive and entertaining in the English Premier League.

Hammers' supporters have had the luxury of witnessing some of the world's top soccer players and managers represent the club over the years, including unforgettable characters such as Ron Greenwood, John Lyall, Syd King, Harry Redknapp, Vic Watson, Geoff Hurst, Bobby Moore, Martin Peters, Phil Parkes, Trevor Brooking, Bryan "Pop" Robson, Tony Cottee, Frank Lampard senior and junior, Julian Dicks, Rio Ferdinand, Paolo Di Canio, Mervyn Day, Shaka Hislop, Clyde Best, Dimitri Payet, Martin Peters, and Alvin Martin.

This trivia and quiz book was put together to celebrate West Ham's colorful history by re-visiting it from day one in 1895 to April 2021. You'll meet many of the club's most influential members and learn how they left their mark on the club.

The Hammers' history is told here in quiz form with 12 unique chapters, each presenting a different topic. All sections feature 20 titillating quiz questions, along with 10 informative "Did You Know" facts. The questions are presented in 15 multiple-choice and 5 true-or-false options, with the answers available on a separate page.

This is an impeccable way to test your knowledge of the famous history of West Ham United, and to challenge other fans of the Hammers in particular, and soccer in general, to quiz showdowns. The book will refresh your memory of your favorite team and help prepare you for any and all trivia challenges that come your way.

CHAPTER 1:

ORIGINS & HISTORY

QUIZ TIME!

1. In what year was the club founded?

    a. 1880

    b. 1884

    c. 1895

    d. 1899

2. Arnold Hills and Dave Taylor were both founders of the club.

    a. True

    b. False

3. The club was founded under what name?

    a. Thames FC

    b. Hammers FC

    c. Thames Ironworks

    d. Shippers Athletic Club

4. What was the first league the side played in?

a. The Southern League

b. The London League

c. The Football League

d. The Western League

5. Which team did the club play their first match against?

a. Chatham Town FC

b. Royal Ordnance FC Reserves

c. Fulham FC

d. Crouch End Vampires FC

6. Which is not one of West Ham's nicknames?

a. The Hammers

b. The Irons

c. The Academy

d. The Sailors

7. West Ham was a founding member of the Premier League.

a. True

b. False

8. What was the outcome of the club's first recorded match?

a. 1-1 draw

b. 5-0 win

c. 0-3 loss

d. 2-1 win

9. What was the team's original kit color?

a. Maroon

b. Navy Blue

c. Oxford blue

d. Claret

10. How many times has West Ham been relegated?

    a. 3

    b. 5

    c. 6

    d. 9

11. What was the first club the Hammers played in their debut in the Football League?

    a. Wolverhampton Wanderers

    b. Blackpool FC

    c. Millwall FC

    d. Lincoln City FC

12. The team played its home games at Boleyn Ground Stadium (Upton Park) between 1904 and 2016.

    a. True

    b. False

13. How many matches did the squad win in its first English Football League season?

    a. 23

    b. 19

    c. 14

    d. 10

14. Which year was West Ham first relegated in the Football League?

a. 1988-89

b. 1977-78

c. 1955-56

d. 1931-32

15. Which side did the Hammers face in their first Premier League outing?

a. Coventry City FC

b. Queens Park Rangers

c. Wimbledon FC

d. Leeds United

16. West Ham's original crest featured two crossed rivet hammers over an anvil.

a. True

b. False

17. How many games did the Hammers win in their first season in the London League?

a. 4

b. 7

c. 9

d. 12

18. West Ham beat which club to win their first Premier League game?

a. Sheffield Wednesday

b. Chelsea FC

c. Blackburn Rovers

d. Manchester United

19. Which player scored West Ham's first Premier League goal?

    a. Clive Allen

    b. Trevor Morley

    c. Lee Chapman

    d. Dale Gordon

20. The Hammers have been relegated in the Premier League era twice.

    a. True

    b. False

QUIZ ANSWERS

1. C – 1895

2. A – True

3. C – Thames Ironworks

4. B – London League

5. B – Royal Ordnance FC Reserves

6. D – The Sailors

7. B – False

8. A – 1-1 draw

9. C – Oxford blue

10. C – 6

11. D – Lincoln City FC

12. A – True

13. B – 19

14. D – 1931-32

15. C – Wimbledon FC

16. B – False

17. B – 7

18. A – Sheffield Wednesday

19. D – Dale Gordon

20. A – True

DID YOU KNOW?

1. West Ham United FC is based in East London, England, and currently competes in the top-tier English Premier League. The club was originally founded in 1895 and is nicknamed the Irons and the Hammers, with The Cockney Boys and the Academy of Football, as less common nicknames. Most neutral fans simply refer to the club as West Ham, which is also an area in London. The team's home ground is London Stadium, which has a capacity of 60,000. The majority shareholder of the club is David Sullivan.

2. The managing director of the Thames Ironworks and Shipbuilding Company, Arnold Hills, was asked by one of his workers if the company could form a soccer team. Hills, a former soccer player and sportsman, had already helped form several other sports clubs and gladly started Thames Ironworks FC in June 1895.

3. The new Thames Ironworks club played several friendly matches in 1895-96, with most of their home matches at nearby Hermit Road. The team's original colors were Oxford blue, with a Union Jack flag added to the kit in 1896-97. Between 1897 and 1900, the colors were changed to red, white, and blue.

4. Francis Payne became the first chairman and director of the club, with Ted Harsent acting as the coach while Tom

Robinson was appointed trainer. The club's first match, played on Sept. 7, 1895, was a 1-1 friendly draw against Southern League team Royal Ordnance Factories FC, which was the reserve squad of Woolwich Arsenal at the time. Arthur Darby was credited with scoring the team's goal.

5. The club's first competitive fixture was played on October 12, 1895 and resulted in a 5-0 defeat by Chatham Town of the Kent League, in the first qualifying round for the FA Cup. Robert Stevenson was listed as the first captain for the Thames Ironworks team that day. Other known players were Walter Parks, Johnny Stewart, George Sage, James Lindsay, and Thomas Freeman.

6. Since Arnold Hills suggested his players refrain from drinking alcohol, the squad's nickname was the Tee-Totallers. The team won the West Ham Charity Cup on April 20, 1896, by beating Barking Woodville in a second replay, and the team won 30 of 46 games played in 1895-96. The club also experimented with night games by placing 2,000 light bulbs, which were suspended by poles around the Hermit Road pitch in December 1895.

7. Thames Ironworks FC joined the seven-team London League in 1896-97 with a kit consisting of Royal Cambridge Blue shirts, white shorts, and red caps, belts, and socks. In September 1896, the club was evicted from the Hermit Road ground, after erecting a fence around the pitch and charging fans admission. The team then moved to a new venue known as Browning Road, but it was unsuitable, so

they relocated in June 1897 to a new 100,000-capacity multi-sports venue that became the Memorial Grounds.

8. The team changed colors again in November 1897 when the kit featured a sky-blue shirt, white shorts, and scarlet socks. A year later, the West Ham rail station opened close to the Memorial Grounds venue. The club won the London League title in 1897-98 by winning 12 of 16 league outings and then turned professional, joining the Southern League in 1898-99. The first season was a success, as the side won the league's Second Division title and was promoted to the First Division.

9. The Thames Ironworks and Shipbuilding Company became a public company, and the soccer club was reorganized in 1900. The team resigned from the Southern League in June 1900 and was rebranded as West Ham United on July 5, 1900, joining the Western League in 1901. The club adopted its claret and sky-blue color scheme in the early 1900s, with the claret shirt, and sky-blue sleeves first showing up in 1903-04.

10. In 1904, the rental agreement at Memorial Gardens was about to expire and the club moved to a new stadium, which was named the Boleyn Ground, but would soon be commonly known as Upton Park. It served as the club's home ground from 1904 to 2016. West Ham didn't join the English Football League until 1919-20 when it was admitted to the Second Division. The Hammers finished as runners-up in 1922-23, reached the FA Cup final, and were promoted to the First Division.

CHAPTER 2:

THE CAPTAIN CLASS

QUIZ TIME!

1. Who captained West Ham in its first Premier League season?

   a. Steve Potts
   b. Julian Dicks
   c. Ian Bishop
   d. Steve Lomas

2. Lucas Neill was the first Hammers captain born outside of Europe.

   a. True
   b. False

3. Nigel Reo-Coker captained which club before joining West Ham?

   a. Fulham FC
   b. Bolton Wanderers
   c. Ipswich Town FC
   d. Wimbledon FC

4. Who did Mark Noble succeed as captain?

   a. Matthew Upson

   b. Kevin Nolan

   c. Lucas Neill

   d. Andy Carroll

5. Which player was the first captain in club history?

   a. William Chapman

   b. Charlie Dove

   c. Robert Stevenson

   d. Johnny Stewart

6. How many FA Cup trophies did Billy Bonds captain the Hammers to?

   a. 7

   b. 5

   c. 2

   d. 3

7. Bobby Moore famously captained the English men's national team to its first FIFA World Cup trophy.

   a. True

   b. False

8. Who captained the Hammers to the Southern League Second Division title in 1898-99?

   a. Frank Piercy

   b. Tom Bradshaw

   c. Ernest Watts

   d. Walter Tranter

9. Christian Dailly left what club to captain West Ham?

    a. Sunderland AFC
    b. Blackburn Rovers
    c. Portsmouth FC
    d. Rangers FC

10. How many times was Noel Cantwell capped by the Republic of Ireland's national team?

    a. 15
    b. 22
    c. 36
    d. 43

11. Who was the first West Ham skipper born outside the British Isles?

    a. Benni McCarthy
    b. Lucas Neill
    c. Paulo Di Canio
    d. Youssef Sofiane

12. George Kay was the Hammers' first captain in the Football League.

    a. True
    b. False

13. Mark Noble was given which nickname?

    a. Sir Noble
    b. Lord of West Ham
    c. Hammer Time
    d. Mr. West Ham

14. Lucas Neill took the captain's armband from which player?

    a. Nigel Reo-Coker
    b. Christian Dailly
    c. Joe Cole
    d. Matthew Upson

15. FHow many matches did Bobby Moore captain the English men's national team?

    a. 90
    b. 74
    c. 66
    d. 52

16. Julian Dicks had two stints as West Ham's captain.

    a. True
    b. False

17. How many games did Lucas Neill captain the Australian men's national team?

    a. 43
    b. 57
    c. 61
    d. 72

18. Who captained the Hammers to their first Football League championship?

    a. Phil Woosnam
    b. Malcolm Allison

c. Alvin Martin

d. Noel Cantwell

19. Who succeeded Julian Dicks as skipper in 1997?

    a. Frank Lampard Sr.

    b. Rio Ferdinand

    c. Steve Lomas

    d. Joe Cole

20. Phil Woosnam captained the Hammers during their first European competition.

    a. True

    b. False

QUIZ ANSWERS

1. A – Steve Potts

2. A – True

3. D – Wimbledon FC

4. B – Kevin Nolan

5. C – Robert Stevenson

6. C – 2

7. A – True

8. D – Walter Tranter

9. B – Blackburn Rovers

10. C – 36

11. C – Paulo Di Canio

12. B – False

13. D – Mr. West Ham

14. A – Nigel Reo-Coker

15. A – 90

16. A – True

17. C – 61

18. D – Noel Cantwell

19. C – Steve Lomas

20. B – False

DID YOU KNOW?

1. The club has appointed approximately 35 full-time captains since being formed in 1895. The first known skipper was Robert Stevenson of Thames Ironworks FC and the latest is midfielder Mark Noble, who was appointed in 2015. All captains have been from the British Isles other than Paolo Di Canio of Italy and Lucas Neill of Australia. The Hammers have had 11 different captains in the Premier League.

2. Robert Stevenson of Scotland could play just about anywhere on the pitch and was the first skipper of Thames Ironworks. He joined the team for its first-ever campaign in 1895-96 from Woolwich Arsenal, where he was often the club's captain. Stevenson is believed to have notched 8 goals in 20 games while helping the side win the West Ham Charity Cup. He then tallied 6 goals in 16 matches in 1896-97 and left the team in February 1897 to return to Scotland and play for Arthurlie.

3. In 1899, forward Thomas "Henry" Bradshaw was appointed team captain after having played for Liverpool and Northwich Victoria and joining Thames Ironworks from Tottenham Hotspur. He had earlier helped hometown Liverpool win two Second Division titles and was the first Liverpool player ever to represent the England National Team. During a Southern League game in October 1899,

Bradshaw received a kick to the head that slowly affected his health. He continued to play but passed away on Christmas Day 1899 at the age of 26.

4. Defender Noel Cantwell arrived at Upton Park from Cork Athletic in 1952 and captained the side to the Second Division title in 1957-58 to place the Hammers back into the top flight, for the first time since 1932. Cantwell was sold to Manchester United in November 1960 for £29,500, a record fee for a full-back at the time. He helped United capture two league titles and wore the armband in the team's 1962-63 FA Cup final win. Cantwell also captained the Republic of Ireland squad on several occasions, played cricket for the Irish national team, later served as chairman of the Professional Footballers' Association, and became a soccer manager.

5. The first West Ham manager from outside the British Isles was Italian forward Paolo Di Canio, who joined in January 1999 from Sheffield Wednesday. In 1999-2000, he was named Hammer of the Year and won the BBC Goal of the Season Award, and the league's Goal of the Decade Award after a Sky Sports viewers' poll. In a match against Everton in December 2000, Di Canio stopped the play and picked up the ball after Everton goalkeeper Paul Gerrard injured himself. FIFA officially recognized Di Canio's gesture and presented him with the FIFA Fair Play Award. West Ham was relegated on the final day of the 2003-04 season and Di Canio joined Charlton Athletic on a free transfer after scoring 51 goals in 141 appearances.

6. the Hammers' first and only skipper to hail from outside of Europe so far was Australian international defender Lucas Neill. He arrived in January 2007 and wore the captain's armband for the first time in March. He was then appointed full-time skipper after Nigel Reo-Coker was transferred to Aston Villa in the summer of 2007. At the end of the 2008-09 season, Neill turned down a one-year contract extension with West Ham to join Everton as a free agent, after just 88 matches with the team. Neill later played in Turkey, the United Arab Emirates, and Japan.

7. English international defender Bobby Moore was a West Ham legend as captain and also skippered his national team to a World Cup trophy in 1966. In fact, there's a statue in his honor outside the new Wembley Stadium in London. Moore was a West Ham youth player, and then starred for the senior side from 1958 to 1974, before joining Fulham. He led the Hammers to the 1963-1964 FA Cup and the 1964-65 European Cup Winners' Cup. Moore was named the FWA Footballer of the Year in 1964 and the Hammer of the Year four times. His No. 6 shirt was retired by the club in 2008 and he received the club's Lifetime Achievement award in 2017. Moore played 647 games with the team and won several other individual awards during his career.

8. Billy Bonds spent 27 years with West Ham as player and manager and holds the club record for appearances at 799. He was Hammer of the Year four times and the runner-up three times. Bonds arrived from Charlton Athletic in May

1967. The defender and midfielder shared the club's scoring lead with Clyde Best in 1973-74 and was appointed captain in March 1974 to succeed Bobby Moore. He helped the team win the 1974-75 FA Cup and reach the final of the 1975-76 European Cup Winners' Cup. He won the FA Cup again in 1979-80, led the side to the 1980-81 League Cup final, and Second Division title. Bonds retired from playing in the summer of 1988 at the age of 41 and managed the Hammers between 1990 and 1994. He was awarded the club's first lifetime achievement award in 2013.

9. When Billy Bonds hung up his boots in May 1984, the captain's armband was given to English international defender Alvin Martin, who had joined the club a decade before as a youth player. He was named Hammer of the Year three times between 1979-80 and 1982-83 while winning the FA Cup in 1979-80 and being named to the PFA Second Division Team of the Year for 1980-81 when the club won the second-tier title. Martin played 596 games with the side before joining Leyton Orient in 1996 for a season before retiring. Martin scored a hat trick against Newcastle United in April 1986 by notching a goal against three different keepers.

10. Midfielder Mark Noble has been with West Ham since his youth days in 2000 but spent some time on loan to Hull City and Ipswich Town in 2006. His loyalty and services to the club have earned him the nickname "Mr. West Ham", and he's played more Premier League matches with the team than anybody else. Noble has won the Hammer of

the Year Award twice and was voted Hammer of the Decade at the end of the 2010s. Noble is an expert penalty-taker, with 27 of his first 28 spot kicks being successful. He's been captain of the club since 2015 and has played over 500 games with the Hammers, scoring 60 goals.

CHAPTER 3:

AMAZING MANAGERS

QUIZ TIME!

1. Who was the club's first full-time manager?

   a. Mac Fleming

   b. Ted Fenton

   c. Syd King

   d. Charlie Paynter

2. The club was managed by a committee between 1895 and 1902.

   a. True

   b. False

3. Alan Pardew managed which team before joining West Ham?

   a. Sunderland AFC

   b. Bristol Rovers

   c. Reading FC

   d. Middlesbrough FC

4. Who won the 1974-75 FA Cup with the club?

a. Billy Bonds

b. Ron Greenwood

c. Syd King

d. John Lyall

5. Who managed West Ham during its first season in the Premier League?

a. Lou Macari

b. Harry Redknapp

c. Glenn Roeder

d. Billy Bonds

6. Which club did Harry Redknapp leave to join the Hammers?

a. Arsenal FC

b. Coventry City FC

c. AFC Bournemouth

d. Queens Park Rangers

7. Harry Redknapp was the longest-serving manager.

a. True

b. False

8. How many European trophies did Ron Greenwood lead West Ham to?

a. 6

b. 4

c. 2

d. 1

9. Which manager led the team to its first Football League title?

    a. John Lyall

    b. Charlie Paynter

    c. Ted Fenton

    d. Ron Greenwood

10. John Lyall left West Ham to manage what outfit?

    a. Newcastle United

    b. Aston Villa

    c. Manchester City

    d. Ipswich Town

11. Who was the Hammers' first manager born outside of the British Isles?

    a. Gianfranco Zola

    b. Avram Grant

    c. Slaven Bilić

    d. Manuel Pellegrini

12. Sam Allardyce led West Ham to a 3rd-place finish in the 2013-14 Premier League.

    a. True

    b. False

13. Who succeeded Harry Redknapp as boss?

    a. Alan Pardew

    b. Glenn Roeder

    c. Trevor Brooking

    d. Kevin Keen

14. Lou Macari took over as manager in July of which year?

    a. 1988

    b. 1989

    c. 1990

    d. 1991

15. Whom did Slaven Bilić replace as manager?

    a. Avram Grant

    b. David Moyes

    c. Sam Allardyce

    d. Alan Curbishley

16. Syd King was appointed the club's boss while still playing with the team.

    a. True

    b. False

17. How many trophies did Manuel Pellegrini win with the Hammers?

    a. 0

    b. 1

    c. 3

    d. 2

18. Who did David Moyes succeed as manager in 2019?

    a. a. Slaven Bilić

    b. Manuel Pellegrini

    c. Sam Allardyce

    d. Avram Grant

19. How many Scottish-born permanent managers has West Ham employed?

    a. 0
    b. 1
    c. 2
    d. 4

20. West Ham has employed seven caretaker managers.

    a. True
    b. False

QUIZ ANSWERS

1. C – Syd King

2. A – True

3. C – Reading FC

4. D – John Lyall

5. D – Billy Bonds

6. C – AFC Bournemouth

7. B – False

8. D – 1

9. C – Ted Fenton

10. D – Ipswich Town

11. A – Gianfranco Zola

12. B – False

13. B – Glenn Roeder

14. B – 1989

15. C – Sam Allardyce

16. A – True

17. A – 0

18. B – Manuel Pellegrini

19. B – 2

20. B – False

DID YOU KNOW?

1. As of April 2021, West Ham has had 17 different full-time managers and three part-time bosses. Current manager David Moyes has held the job twice. Between 1895 and 1902, team selection was handled by a committee. It's believed that Lee Bowen served as the club's secretary in 1900-01 with Syd King becoming the first official manager in 1902.

2. The first 11 full-time managers were all British, 10 of them were English and the other, Lou Macari, hailed from Scotland. In all, there have been 11 full-time managers from England, two from Scotland (Macari and David Moyes), one from Italy (Gianfranco Zola), one from Israel (Avram Grant), one from Croatia (Slaven Bilić), and one from Chile (Manuel Pellegrini).

3. Here is the full list of full-time and caretaker managers: Syd King 1902-32, Charlie Paynter 1932-50, Ted Fenton 1950-61, Ron Greenwood 1961-74, John Lyall 1974-89, Lou Macari 1989-90, Ronnie Boyce 1990, Billy Bonds 1990-94, Harry Redknapp 1994-2001, Glenn Roeder 2001-03, Trevor Brooking 2003, Alan Pardew 2003-06, Alan Curbishley 2006-08, Kevin Keen 2008, Gianfranco Zola 2008-10, Avram Grant 2010-11, Kevin Keen 2011, Sam Allardyce 2011-15, Slaven Bilić 2015-17, David Moyes 2017-18, Manuel Pellegrini 2018-19, David Moyes 2019-present.

4. Syd King spent just over 30 years as the club's first full-time manager after joining as a player in 1899 when it was Thames Ironworks. He was appointed manager in 1902 and saw the side move to Upton Park in 1904, then join the English Football League in 1919. He was in charge when the team earned promotion to the First Division and reached its first FA Cup final in 1923. King was made a shareholder of the club in 1931 but left in November 1932, after being relegated a few months earlier. Sadly, King took his own life in February 1933 at the age of 59. He was in charge for 638 games with a record of 248 wins, 146 draws, 244 losses, and a 38.87 winning percentage.

5. Ron Greenwood of England was appointed boss in April 1961 and guided the club to its first major trophies. The former player led the side to the 1963-64 FA Cup and 1964-65 European Cup Winners' Cup as well as sharing the 1964 FA Charity Shield. After 13 years, he became the club's general manager in August 1974, while his assistant John Lyall took over as manager. Greenwood became the manager of England's National Team in 1977 and was later inducted into the English Football Hall of Fame. He managed 658 Hammers' games and won 35.87 percent of them.

6. The manager with the most Hammer games under his belt is John Lyall of England. He was in charge for 770 contests and won 40 percent of them between August 1974 and June 1989. The former West Ham defender retired from playing in 1963 due to a knee injury. He guided the side to

the 1974-75 FA Cup and 1975-76 European Cup Winners' Cup final. His squad was relegated to the second tier in 1978, reached another FA Cup final in 1979-1980, won the 1980-81 Second Division title, and reached the League Cup final the same season. The club was relegated again in 1989 and, after 34 years with the team, Lyall joined Ipswich Town.

7. Lou Macari, who followed John Lyall as manager in July 1989, was the first to hail from Scotland. He also had the shortest reign as a full-time West Ham boss as he lasted under 40 games and seven months. The former international striker took over just after the club had been relegated to the second tier. He suddenly resigned in February 1990 after an English newspaper alleged that he was involved in betting and illegal payments to players while managing at Swindon Town. Macari resumed his managerial career a year later with Birmingham City.

8. Alan Curbishley of England started his playing career with the Hammers from 1975 to 1979 and finished it as player-coach with Charlton Athletic. He was appointed West Ham manager in December 2006 and managed to avoid relegation by winning seven of nine games toward the end of the season. Curbishley's squad finished the 2007-08 campaign in 10th place in the Premier League. However, he resigned from the club in September 2008 after a disagreement regarding transfers, and became a television pundit. Curbishley later won a lawsuit against the club regarding his resignation. His brother Bill Curbishley

managed rock musicians such as The Who, Judas Priest, Jimmy Page, and Robert Plant.

9. The first non-British manager at Upton Park was former Italian international forward Gianfranco Zola. He took the job in September 2008 after winning numerous team trophies as a player and being named the Footballer of the Year in 2007. His West Ham side finished ninth in the Premier League in 2008-09 but struggled the following campaign by winning just eight league outings to finish 17th in the table. Zola left the club soon afterward. He managed 80 games with the club and had a record of 23 wins, 21 draws, and 36 defeats for a 28.75 winning percentage.

10. Scotsman David Moyes was appointed manager in November 2017 after making a name for himself as boss of Everton but then struggling somewhat at Manchester United, Real Sociedad, and Sunderland. The former player helped the Hammers avoid relegation in 2017-18 by finishing in 13th place in the Premier League but wasn't offered a new contract at the end of the season after winning just 9 of 31 games. Moyes was re-hired by the Hammers on Dec. 29, 2019. to replace Manuel Pellegrini. The team finished 16th in the league and Moyes was still in charge in 2020-21.

CHAPTER 4:

GOALTENDING GREATS

QUIZ TIME!

1. Which keeper played the most games with the club?

    a. David James
    b. Phil Parkes
    c. Ted Hufton
    d. Luděk Mikloško

2. Seven different keepers made an appearance in the 1999-00 Premier League season.

    a. True
    b. False

3. How many clean sheets did Stephen Bywater keep in the 2004-05 Championship League season?

    a. 12
    b. 9
    c. 5
    d. 1

4. Which player backed up Darren Randolph in 16 matches in the 2016-17 domestic league campaign?

    a. Łukasz Fabiański
    b. Jussi Jääskeläinen
    c. David Martin
    d. Adrián

5. Rob Green joined the Hammers from which club?

    a. Fulham FC
    b. Huddersfield Town FC
    c. Norwich City FC
    d. Leeds United

6. Which keeper was named Hammer of the Year for 1998-99?

    a. Manuel Almunia
    b. Péter Kurucz
    c. Shaka Hislop
    d. Ruud Boffin

7. Luděk Mikloško played in West Ham's first-ever Premier League game.

    a. True
    b. False

8. David James left West Ham to join which side?

    a. Borussia Dortmund
    b. Liverpool FC
    c. AC Milan
    d. Manchester City FC

9. For how many years was keeper and coach Ernie Gregory associated with the Hammers?

    a. 8
    b. 15
    c. 34
    d. 51

10. Who appeared in 34 games in the 2000-01 domestic league?

    a. David James
    b. Pavel Srníček
    c. Craig Forest
    d. Shaka Hislop

11. How many clean sheets did Shaka Hislop record in the 1998-99 Premier League season?

    a. 17
    b. 15
    c. 11
    d. 8

12. Joe Hart was loaned to the Hammers by Torino FC for the 2017-18 domestic league season.

    a. True
    b. False

13. Phil Parkes left what club to join West Ham?

    a. Crystal Palace FC
    b. Brighton and Hove Albion
    c. Sunderland AFC
    d. Queens Park Rangers

14. How many official non-wartime appearances did Ted Hufton make with the team?

    a. 456
    b. 433
    c. 402
    d. 376

15. Which player appeared in 27 games in the 2003-04 domestic league season?

    a. Shaka Hislop
    b. Pavel Srníček
    c. David James
    d. Stephen Bywater

16. Luděk Miklóško was capped 42 times by the Czechoslovakia/Czech Republic.

    a. True
    b. False

17. From which club did Łukasz Fabiański join West Ham?

    a. Swansea City FC
    b. Legia Warsaw
    c. Aston Villa
    d. Lech Poznań

18. How many clean sheets did Rob Green post in the 2011-12 Championship League season?

    a. 7
    b. 10

c. 14

d. 17

19. How many appearances did Phil Parkes make in all competitions with West Ham?

   a. 462

   b. 457

   c. 444

   d. 359

20. Jussi Jääskeläinen played all 38 matches in the 2012-13 domestic league season.

   a. True

   b. False

QUIZ ANSWERS

1. B – Phil Parkes

2. B – False

3. A – 12

4. D – Adrián

5. C – Norwich City FC

6. C – Shaka Hislop

7. A – True

8. D – Manchester City FC

9. D – 51

10. D – Shaka Hislop

11. B – 15

12. B – False

13. D – Queens Park Rangers

14. C – 402

15. C – David James

16. A – True

17. A – Swansea City FC

18. D – 17

19. C – 444

20. A – True

DID YOU KNOW?

1. West Ham goalkeepers who have been honored with the Hammer of the Year Award are 1962 Lawrie Leslie, 1981 Phil Parkes, 1991 Luděk Mikloško, 1999 Shaka Hislop, 2008 Robert Green, and 2019 Łukasz Fabiański.

2. With 146 clean sheets in 444 appearances, Phil Parkes was one of the club's longest serving, and most effective keepers. He arrived from Queens Park Rangers in 1979 for £565,000, then a world record for a keeper. Parkes helped the side win the 1979-80 FA Cup and followed up the next season by capturing the Second Division crown. He was named Hemmer of the Year for 1980-81 and to the FA Second Division Team of the Year for 1979-80. Parkes joined Ipswich Town in 1990 on a free transfer and retired soon afterward.

3. Although he was also a professional cricket player with Worcestershire, Jim Standen's finest sporting moments came as West Ham keeper. He played between the posts when the club won the 1963-64 FA Cup and the 1964-65 European Cup Winners' Cup while sharing the 1965 FA Charity Shield. He joined the side in 1962 from Luton Town as an emergency signing when Lawrie Leslie broke a leg. After more than 240 appearances with the Hammers, Standen lost his starting job and left to play in America in 1967. He returned to play out his career in England and

then went back to America, where he became goalkeeper coach at Fresno State University for a spell.

4. Czech Republic international Luděk Mikloško signed from his homeland in February 1990. He played every league game in 1990-91, and 56 overall when the team earned promotion as runners-up in the Second Division. He was the recipient of the season's Hammer of the Year Award and conceded just 16 away goals in the league campaign. The cult hero helped the team earn promotion again in 1992-93 after they had been relegated again the previous season. Mikloško appeared in over 350 games before joining Queens Park Rangers in 1998.

5. Still with the club in April 2021 was Polish international Łukasz Fabiański, who arrived from Swansea City in June 2018, for a reported £7 million. He signed a three-year contract and became the first Polish player with the senior side. He was quite impressive in 2018-19 and was named the Hammer of the Year for his performances after appearing in every league outing. He then extended his contract until June 2022. Fabiański was still the first-choice keeper in 2020-21 and was closing in on 100 appearances with the side.

6. One of the club's finest keepers in the Premier League era was English international Rob Green, who arrived in 2006 from Norwich City. He helped the team avoid relegation in 2006-07 by posting five clean sheets in the final eight games of the season. He saved the first three penalty kicks he faced in 2007-08 and won the season's Hammer of the

Year Award. Green was the first-choice keeper for six straight seasons, but the Hammers were relegated in 2011. He helped them earn promotion the following year by winning the 2012 Championship League playoffs. Green joined Queen's Park Rangers on a free transfer in 2012 after nearly 250 games with West Ham.

7. Adrián San Miguel del Castillo, commonly known as Adrián, was basically an unknown quantity when he joined West Ham in 2013 from Real Betis, in his homeland of Spain. However, he soon won the fans over with his shot-stopping abilities. He won several team awards in his first campaign, including Save of the Season, Best Individual Performance, and Signing of the Season. In addition, he finished as runner-up in the Hammer of the Year voting. He played all 38 league matches in 2014-15 and appeared in 150 contests overall before being released in 2019. Adrián then joined Liverpool on a free transfer.

8. Mervyn Day kicked off his pro career with the Hammers from 1973 to 1979 after arriving as a youth player. In May 1975, he became the youngest keeper to play in an FA Cup final at just 19 years old when he shut out Fulham. He won the PFA Young Player of the Year Award the same season, to become the first keeper ever to receive it. Day played in the 1975-76 European Cup Winners' Cup final defeat to Anderlecht, but he soon struggled with injuries and a loss of form. He was sold to Leyton Orient for a reported £100,000 in 1979 but returned to the Hammers in 2006 as assistant manager.

9. Although he was born in England, Shaka Hislop played internationally with Trinidad & Tobago. He arrived on a free transfer in 1998 from Newcastle United and won the Hammer of the Year Award for his play during his first season. However, he broke his leg in his second campaign to prematurely end his season, and manager Glenn Roeder acquired keeper David James. Hislop remained the first-choice keeper after James tore his knee ligaments before the 2001-02 season but joined Portsmouth in July 2002 on a free transfer. He returned in July 2005 and helped the side reach the 2005-06 FA Cup final before leaving to play in America two months later.

10. Ernie Gregory spent a remarkable 51 years with West Ham after arriving from Leytonstone FC as he made his debut in 1938 and remained until 1987. He actually started on the ground staff and played with the club's boys' team. Gregory went on to make more than 400 official appearances as a senior side keeper over 21 years. However, his career was interrupted by World War II. Gregory then hung up his boots in 1959 and became a first-team and reserve team coach and later was named an administrator. As a player, he helped the side win the Second Division title in 1957-58.

CHAPTER 5:

DARING DEFENDERS

QUIZ TIME!

1. Who appeared in the most career games with the Hammers?

   a. Steve Potts
   b. Alvin Martin
   c. Bobby Moore
   d. Frank Lampard Sr.

2. Tomáš Řepka was shown 14 yellow cards in the 2003-04 domestic league season.

   a. True
   b. False

3. How many goals did Issa Diop score in the 2019-20 Premier League?

   a. 8
   b. 6
   c. 3
   d. 1

4. Who made 36 appearances in all competitions in 2009-10?

    a. Jonathan Spector
    b. Radoslav Kováč
    c. Matthew Upson
    d. Julien Faubert

5. Which player tallied 5 goals in the 2015-16 Premier League?

    a. Aaron Cresswell
    b. Cheikhou Kouyaté
    c. Carl Jenkinson
    d. Winston Reid

6. How many appearances did Bobby Moore make in all competitions with West Ham?

    a. 593
    b. 612
    c. 647
    d. 677

7. Alvin Martin was capped 20 times by the English men's national team.

    a. True
    b. False

8. Steve Potts left West Ham to join which team?

    a. Dagenham and Redbridge FC
    b. Stoke City FC
    c. Fulham FC
    d. Crystal Palace

9. How many goals did James Tomkins score in all competitions in 2011-12?

    a. 4

    b. 7

    c. 2

    d. 9

10. Which player made 44 appearances in all competitions in 2007-08?

    a. Anton Ferdinand

    b. Matthew Upson

    c. Lucas Neill

    d. George McCartney

11. How many appearances did Alvin Martin make for the club in all competitions?

    a. 560

    b. 587

    c. 596

    d. 624

12. Aaron Cresswell tallied 7 assists in all competitions in 2014-15.

    a. True

    b. False

13. Which player scored twice in the 2012-13 domestic league?

    a. Winston Reid

    b. Joey O'Brien

c. James Tomkins

d. Guy Demel

14. Which player appeared in 41 games for West Ham in the 1993-94 Premier League?

    a. Tony Gale

    b. Steve Potts

    c. Tim Breacker

    d. David Burrows

15. How many appearances did Frank Lampard Sr. make in all competitions for the Hammers?

    a. 573

    b. 661

    c. 670

    d. 692

16. Bobby Moore won the FWA Footballer of the Year award in 1963-64.

    a. True

    b. False

17. Which player scored 3 goals in all competitions in 2017-18?

    a. Angelo Ogbonna

    b. Aaron Cresswell

    c. Cheikhou Kouyaté

    d. Arthur Masuaku

18. How many yellow cards was Stuart Pearce shown in the 2000-01 domestic league?

a. 15

b. 11

c. 8

d. 7

19. Which club did Arthur Masuaku leave to join West Ham?

    a. Toulouse FC

    b. Amiens SC

    c. Ipswich Town FC

    d. Olympiacos FC

20. Paul Koncheskey was shown 3 red cards in the 2005-06 domestic league season.

    a. True

    b. False

QUIZ ANSWERS

1. D – Frank Lampard Sr.

2. A - True

3. C – 3

4. D – Julien Faubert

5. B – Cheikhou Kouyaté

6. C – 647

7. B – False

8. A – Dagenham and Redbridge FC

9. A – 4

10. D – George McCartney

11. C – 596

12. A – True

13. B – Joey O'Brien

14. B – Steve Potts

15. C – 670

16. A – True

17. A – Angelo Ogbonna

18. C – 8

19. D – Olympiacos FC

20. B – False

DID YOU KNOW?

1. West Ham defenders who have won the Hammer of the Year Award are, 1961 Bobby Moore, 1963 Bobby Moore, 1968 Bobby Moore, 1970 Bobby Moore, 1971 Billy Bonds 1974 Billy Bonds, 1975 Billy Bonds, 1980 Alvin Martin, 1982 Alvin Martin, 1983 Alvin Martin, 1987 Billy Bonds, 1990 Julian Dicks, 1992 Julian Dicks, 1993 Steve Potts, 1995 Steve Potts, 1996 Julian Dicks, 1997 Julian Dicks, 1998 Rio Ferdinand, 2001 Stuart Pearce, 2002 Sébastien Schemmel, 2006 Danny Gabbidon, 2013 Winston Reid, and 2015 Aaron Cresswell.

2. English international Stuart Pearce had carved out a well-deserved reputation as one of the best defenders in the game with Wealdstone, Coventry City, Nottingham Forest, and Newcastle United, before joining the Hammers in 1999. He played just 50 times for the club but was named Hammer of the Year for 2000-01. Pearce, who was nicknamed "Psycho", then joined Manchester City in the summer of 2001. He turned to football management after playing and held jobs with several teams including England. Pearce later returned to West Ham as a first-team coach.

3. Steve Potts was a versatile defender who could play anywhere in the back four and was rewarded for his fine play by winning the Hammer of the Year Award for the 1992-93 and 1994-95 seasons, as well as finishing as

runner-up on two occasions. He joined the club as a youth player and played for the senior side from 1985 to 2002, before joining Dagenham & Redbridge. He was one game short of making 400 league appearances for the Hammers and, perhaps remarkably, was held to just 1 goal. Potts played over 500 total games and wore the captain's armband between 1993 and 1996. He returned to the team as a coach after hanging up his boots.

4. Czech Republic international Tomáš Řepka arrived in 2001 from Fiorentina, and played until 2006, when he joined Sparta Prague. He helped the team win the 2005 Championship League playoffs before leaving and won several team and individual awards with other clubs. Řepka was known for his fiery temper and received 20 red cards during his career. He attacked game officials and a TV cameraman in 2007, and in 2018 he was sentenced to six months in jail for advertising sexual services in the name of his ex-wife on the internet. The sentence was suspended, but in February 2019 he was sentenced to 15 months for fraud, and nine months for driving under the influence.

5. Julian "The Terminator" Dicks was a tenacious defender and influential skipper who won the Hammer of the Year Award four times. He played over 300 games for the squad and contributed 65 goals, 35 of them on successful penalty kicks. Dicks was a West Ham legend who took over in goal in a 1995 game when Luděk Mikloško was sent off. He joined from Birmingham City in 1988 and left for Liverpool in 1993. Dicks returned to the Hammers

after one season and remained until 1999. He helped West Ham earn promotion by finishing as Second Division runners-up in 1990-91 and 1992-93 and later managed the West Ham United Ladies' side.

6. Frank Lampard Sr. may not be as well-known as his son Frank Jr. to the younger generation, but he was a Hammers legend. He appeared in 670 games and scored 22 goals during his 18-year spell with the claret and blue. He graduated from the youth system, made his senior debut in 1967, playing at least 40 games in six straight seasons between 1969-70 and 1975-76. Lampard helped the side win the 1974-75 FA Cup and scored a famous extra-time goal against Everton in the 1979-80 FA Cup semifinal to help the side capture the cup against Arsenal in the final. He also helped the team reach the 1975-76 European Cup Winners Cup and win the 1980-81 Second Division crown. Lampard Sr. ranks second on the Hammers' all-time appearance list to Billy Bonds. He joined Southend United in 1985 but returned to West Ham as assistant manager to Harry Redknapp between 1994 and 2001.

7. Former Hammers manager Slaven Bilić also played for the club before becoming its boss between 2015 and 2017. In fact, he enjoyed a 14-year pro career that also included stints at Hajduk Split, Karlsruher SC, and Everton. He joined Hajduk when he was just 9 years old, and arrived at Upton Park in January 1996, from his homeland. Bilić played just one full season, though, and helped the side finish eighth in the Premier League in 1997-98. After 54

games, he joined Everton before finishing his playing career in Croatia. He then managed several teams including Croatia and West Ham as well as squads in Turkey, Saudi Arabia, and China.

8. English Football Hall of Fame inductee Rio Ferdinand won numerous team and individual awards during his career. But let's not forget it began with West Ham, where he helped the side win its section of the 1999 UEFA Intertoto Cup and was named Hammer of the Year for 1997-98 when he was 19 years old. Ferdinand progressed through the youth-team ranks and made his senior debut in May 1996. He was loaned to Bournemouth for part of 1996-97, then sold to Leeds United in November 2000 for £18 million, which set what was then a British transfer record. Ferdinand's brother Anton also played for West Ham, and his cousins Kane and Leas, were also pro soccer players.

9. New Zealand international skipper Winston Reid was on loan with Brentford in 2020-21 after playing with Sporting Kansas City in America for part of 2020. He joined West Ham in 2010 from FC Midtjylland in Denmark. He was named Hammer of the Year for 2012-13 and the New Zealand Footballer of the Year for 2014. Reid played at the under-19, -20, and -21 levels with Denmark because he possesses Danish citizenship but later switched his international allegiance to his birth nation. Reid has appeared in just over 220 games with West Ham, with 10 goals scored.

10. The winner of the 2005-06 Hammer of the Year Award was Welsh international Danny Gabbidon. He arrived in July 2005 from Cardiff City. He helped the squad reach the 2005-06 FA Cup final and then avoid relegation in 2006-07 when he was sidelined for much of the campaign due to injuries. He sat on the sidelines between December 2007 and August 2009 and was eventually released in June 2011 when he joined Queens Park Rangers. Gabbidon played just over 100 games with the Hammers and later managed Wales as caretaker and became a radio pundit.

CHAPTER 6:

MAESTROS OF THE MIDFIELD

QUIZ TIME!

1. Who made the most appearances for the Hammers in all competitions?

    a. Paul Ince
    b. Alan Devonshire
    c. Billy Bonds
    d. Trevor Brooking

2. Frank Lampard Jr. was the only West Ham player shown a red card in the 1999-00 domestic league.

    a. True
    b. False

3. How many goals did Mark Noble score in the 2013-14 Premier League?

    a. 2
    b. 4
    c. 7
    d. 10

4. Which player appeared in 32 games in the 1997-98 domestic league?

   a. Andy Impey

   b. Stan Lazaridis

   c. Frank Lampard Jr.

   d. Steve Lomas

5. Scott Parker joined the Hammers from which side?

   a. AFC Bournemouth

   b. Fulham FC

   c. Wigan Athletic

   d. Newcastle United

6. How many appearances did Alan Devonshire make in all competitions?

   a. 641

   b. 597

   c. 447

   d. 425

7. Luís Boa Morte tallied 5 assists in all competitions in 2007-08.

   a. True

   b. False

8. Which player scored 9 goals in the 2018-19 Premier League season?

   a. Carlos Sánchez

   b. Jack Wilshere

c. Felipe Anderson

d. Pedro Obiang

9. Billy Bonds left which club to join West Ham?

   a. Preston North End

   b. Charlton Athletic

   c. Millwall FC

   d. Leyton Orient FC

10. Who appeared in 46 games in all competitions in 2015-16?

   a. Alex Song

   b. Pedro Obiang

   c. Victor Moses

   d. Mark Noble

11. How many goals did Scott Parker tally in the 2010-11 domestic league?

   a. 3

   b. 5

   c. 8

   d. 11

12. Édouard Cissé was shown 11 yellow cards in the 2002-03 Premier League.

   a. True

   b. False

13. How many appearances did Trevor Brooking make in all competitions for West Ham?

   a. 757

   b. 742

c. 643

d. 586

14. Which player appeared in 39 games in all competitions in 2019-20?

    a. Declan Rice
    b. Felipe Anderson
    c. Tomáš Souček
    d. Carlos Sánchez

15. How many goals did Frank Lampard Jr. score in the 1999-00 domestic league?

    a. 4
    b. 7
    c. 9
    d. 13

16. Billy Bonds was capped 33 times by the English national team.

    a. True
    b. False

17. Who scored 3 goals in all competitions in 2006-07?

    a. Luís Boa Morte
    b. Matthew Etherington
    c. Nigel Reo-Coker
    d. Hayden Mullins

18. How many appearances did Billy Bonds make in all competitions with the Hammers?

a. a. 813

b. 799

c. 768

d. 647

19. Which player scored 6 goals in all competitions in 2011-12?

   a. Henri Lansbury

   b. Matthew Taylor

   c. Jack Collison

   d. Gary O'Neil

20. Trevor Brooking scored 5 goals for the English men's national team.

   a. True

   b. False

QUIZ ANSWERS

1. C – Billy Bonds

2. B – False

3. B – 4

4. D – Steve Lomas

5. D – Newcastle United

6. C – 447

7. A – True

8. C – Felipe Anderson

9. B – Charlton Athletic

10. D – Mark Noble

11. B – 5

12. B – False

13. C – 643

14. A – Declan Rice

15. B – 7

16. B – False

17. D – Hayden Mullins

18. B – 799

19. C – Jack Collison

20. A – True

DID YOU KNOW?

1. Midfielders who have won the Hammer of the Year Award are 1958 Andy Malcolm, 1959 Ken Brown, 1965 Martin Peters, 1972 Trevor Brooking, 1976 Trevor Brooking, 1977 Trevor Brooking, 1978 Trevor Brooking, 1979 Alan Devonshire, 1984 Trevor Brooking, 1985 Paul Allen, 1988 Stewart Robson, 1989 Paul Ince, 2003 Joe Cole, 2004 Matthew Etherington, 2009 Scott Parker, 2020 Scott Parker, 2022 Scott Parker, 2012 Mark Noble, 2014 Mark Noble, 2016 Dimitri Payet, 2020 Declan Rice.

2. Former skipper Nigel Reo-Coker joined the team from Wimbledon in January 2004, leading the side to the Premier League by winning the 2005 Championship League playoffs. He then guided the squad to the 2005-06 FA Cup final. In 2006-07, the club struggled in the Premier League but managed to avoid relegation on the final day of the season after manager Alan Pardew was fired and replaced by Alan Curbishley. Reo-Coker then requested a transfer and joined Aston Villa for a reported fee of £8.5 million. He played 142 games for the Hammers, contributed 11 goals, and received 33 yellow cards.

3. Frank Lampard Jr. followed in his father's footsteps by signing with the club as a youth. He made his senior debut

in 1996, was sent on loan to Swansea City for a spell, and had become a key player by 1998-1999, when he helped the team finish in fifth place and enter the Intertoto Cup. Lampard played just under 200 games for the Hammers before joining Chelsea in June 2001. Frank's uncle, Harry Redknapp, was West Ham manager while he was at the club and his father was Redknapp's assistant. Lampard is currently the highest-scoring midfielder in Premier League history, Chelsea's all-time leading scorer, one of England's greatest internationals, and the winner of numerous team and individual awards. He later turned to football management.

4. Michael Carrick was another West Ham youth player who became a reliable England international. He helped the club capture the 1988-99 FA Youth Cup before making his senior debut the same season. He was loaned out for brief stints in 1999-2000 and became a regular starter in 2000-2001when he played 41 times in all competitions. He suffered a groin injury in 2002-03 and the team was relegated. Carrick was named to the PFA First Division Team of the Year for 2003-04 and helped the club reach the playoffs but the side was beaten by Crystal Palace. He then joined Tottenham in August 2004.

5. After winning seven trophies with Anderlecht, Senegal international Cheikhou Kouyaté left Belgium for West Ham in June 2014. In his first campaign, he won the club's Individual Performance of the Season Award and played 31 of 38 league games. In March 2016, he signed a new

five-year contract and was sent off twice during the 2015-16 campaign only to have both cards rescinded by the Football Association. On Aug. 4, 2016, Kouyaté made history by scoring the club's first goal at their new London Stadium home in a Europa League contest against NK Domžale. He played just under 150 games before joining Crystal Palace for a reported £9.5 million in 2018.

6. West Ham paid just £5,000 to acquire Alan Devonshire from non-league Southall in September 1976, and it turned out to be one of the best deals they ever made. Devonshire went on to play 14 years for the club, scoring 32 goals in 448 appearances. He formed an excellent partnership with Trevor Brooking and quickly became a key player. He helped the squad win the 1979-80 FA Cup and the Second Division title the following season. West Ham also reached the 1980-81 League Cup final. He missed most of 1984-85 due to injury and the English international joined Watford in 1990. Devonshire had a racehorse named after him and his father Les was also a pro soccer player.

7. English international Trevor Brooking made his West Ham debut at the age of 18 in 1967 and went on to tally 102 goals in 647 games before departing in 1984. He was named Hammer of the Year a record five times and voted runner-up three times. He was the recipient of the club's Lifetime Achievement Award in 2014 and took over as caretaker manager in 2003. Brooking won the FA Cup in 1974-75 and 1979-80 while scoring the winner in the latter. He won the

Second Division title in 1980-81 as well as a European Cup Winners' Cup runners-up medal in 1975-76 and a League Cup runners-up medal in 1980-81. He became Sir Trevor Brooking in 2004 when he was knighted and has a stand named after him at the club's stadium.

8. Kicking off his pro career with the Hammers in 1962 was another fine English international, Martin Peters, who had joined the club as a 15-year-old. The versatile Peters played every position at least once, including goalkeeper. He helped the side win the European Cup Winners' Cup in 1964-65 and was named Hammer of the Year. He helped the side reach the League Cup final in 1965-66 and became a national hero when he scored in England's 1966 World Cup final victory over West Germany. He scored 24 goals in 1968-69 and tallied 100 times overall in 364 games for the club before joining Tottenham Hotspur in 1970 in a deal that saw Jimmy Greaves head to Upton Park. Peters later became a West Ham ambassador.

9. Paul Ince grew up as a Hammers supporter and joined the club at the age of 14 as a trainee. He made his senior debut in November 1986 and became a regular starter in 1987-88, while Billy Bonds was at the end of his West Ham career. Ince was named Hammer of the Year and helped the team reach the League Cup semi-finals in 1988-89, but it was relegated at the end of the season. Ince then joined Manchester United in September 1989 after playing one game in the Second Division. He scored 12 goals in 95 West Ham games and went on to play 53 times

for England and win numerous team and individual awards later in his career before turning to football management.

10. Arriving at West Ham in the summer of 2007 from Newcastle United was English international Scott Parker. He quickly became a fan favorite and won the Hammer of the Year Award three straight seasons, from 2008-09 to 2010-11. In 2010, Parker signed a new five-year contract which reportedly made him the highest-paid player in the club's history. He was named the FWA Footballer of the Year for 2010-11 and the England Player of the Year for 2011. Parker scored 12 times in 129 appearances and wore the captain's armband on several occasions before joining Tottenham Hotspur in August 2011 after West Ham was relegated.

CHAPTER 7:

SENSATIONAL STRIKERS/FORWARDS

QUIZ TIME!

1. Who made more appearances for West Ham?

    a. Jimmy Ruffell

    b. Vic Watson

    c. John Dick

    d. Geoff Hurst

2. Kevin Nolan was shown 2 red cards in the 2013-14 domestic league season.

    a. True

    b. False

3. Which player appeared in 42 matches in all competitions in 1999-00?

    a. Paulo Wanchope

    b. Paul Kitson

    c. Trevor Sinclair

    d. Paolo Di Canio

4. How many goals did Marlon Harewood score in the 2004-05 domestic league season?

   a. 21

   b. 17

   c. 14

   d. 10

5. Which player netted 8 goals in the 2017-18 Premier League?

   a. Manuel Lanzini

   b. Andy Carroll

   c. Javier Hernández (Chicharito)

   d. André Ayew

6. Who made 30 appearances in the 2009-10 domestic league?

   a. Zavon Hines

   b. Junior Stanislas

   c. Alessandro Diamanti

   d. Carlton Cole

7. John Dick was the first West Ham player to make an appearance for the Scottish men's national team.

   a. True

   b. False

8. Which club did Teddy Sheringham leave to join the Hammers?

   a. Tottenham Hotspur

   b. Colchester United

c. Manchester City FC

d. Portsmouth FC

9. How many appearances did Geoff Hurst make in all competitions for West Ham?

   a. 487

   b. 502

   c. 535

   d. 586

10. Which Hammer notched 7 goals in the 2019-20 Premier League?

    a. Robert Snodgrass

    b. Sébastien Haller

    c. Andriy Yarmolenko

    d. Pablo Fornals

11. Who scored 7 goals in the 2006-07 domestic league season?

    a. Kepa Blanco

    b. Marlon Harewood

    c. Carlos Tevez

    d. Yossi Benayoun

12. Geoff Hurst made 49 appearances for the English men's national team.

    a. True

    b. False

13. How many goals did Carlton Cole score in the 2010-11 domestic league?

a. 3

b. 5

c. 8

d. 11

14. From which club did Manuel Lanzini join the Hammers?

    a. FC Shakhtar Donetsk

    b. Al Jazira Club

    c. CA River Plate

    d. Notts County FC

15. How many appearances did Jimmy Ruffell make in all competitions for the Hammers?

    a. 603

    b. 572

    c. 548

    d. 523

16. Enner Valencia tallied 7 assists in all competitions in 2014-15.

    a. True

    b. False

17. Which player scored 9 goals in the 1994-95 Premier League?

    a. Don Hutchison

    b. Jeroen Boere

    c. Michael Hughes

    d. Trevor Morley

18. How many appearances did Vic Watson make for the club in all competitions?

    a. 550
    b. 537
    c. 505
    d. 488

19. Which club Dimitri Payet leave to join West Ham?

    a. FC Bordeaux
    b. AS Saint-Étienne
    c. Olympique Marseille
    d. Aston Villa

20. André Ayew won the 2018-19 Hammer of the Year Award.

    a. True
    b. False

QUIZ ANSWERS

1. A – Jimmy Ruffell

2. A – True

3. D – Paolo Di Canio

4. B – 17

5. C – Javier Hernández (Chicharito)

6. D – Carlton Cole

7. A – True

8. D – Portsmouth FC

9. B – 502

10. B – Sébastien Haller

11. C – Carlos Tevez

12. A – True

13. D – 11

14. B – Al Jazira Club

15. C – 548

16. B – False

17. A – Don Hutchison

18. C – 505

19. C – Olympique Marseille

20. B – False

DID YOU KNOW?

1. Club forwards who have taken home the Hammer of the Year Award are: 1960 Malcolm Musgrove, 1964 Johnny Byrne, 1966 Geoff Hurst, 1967 Geoff Hurst, 1969 Geoff Hurst, 1973 Bryan "Pop" Robson, 1986 Tony Cottee, 1994 Trevor Morley, 2000 Paolo Di Canio, 2005 Teddy Sheringham, 2007 Carlos Tevez, 2017 Michail Antonio, and 2018 Marko Arnautović.

2. After graduating from the youth ranks, John Sissons played 263 games for the Hammers between 1963-1970, contributing 53 goals before joining Sheffield Wednesday, and later playing for Norwich City, Chelsea, then moving on to play in South Africa and America. He became the youngest player to score in a FA Cup final in 1963-64 at the age of 18 and then helped the side win the European Cup Winners' Cup the next season. He also won a runners-up medal at the 1965-66 League Cup final and shared the Charity Shield in 1964. The young winger played for England as a youth but was never capped by the senior side.

3. Although his West Ham career was relatively short, Vic Keeble proved to be one of the side's most prolific scorers with 51 goals in just 84 games. That included 19 league goals in 1957-58 to help the Hammers capture the Second Division title. He joined the club from Newcastle United

for £10,000 in October 1957, scored in his home debut, and notched a hat trick in his fifth outing. By the end of his first campaign, Keeble had netted 24 goals in all competitions. He scored 21 the next season in the top flight. He was forced to retire in 1960 at the age of 30 due to a back injury.

4. Scottish international Frank McAvennie joined the Hammers in 1985 from St. Mirren as a midfielder but was soon converted to a striker. That proved to be a shrewd move, as he tallied 60 goals in 190 games during his two stints. He formed a fine partnership with Tony Cottee and bagged 26 goals in his first season with the side when West Ham finished third in the top tier. However, he joined hometown team Glasgow Celtic after just two years at Upton Park. McAvennie returned in March 1989, though, and helped the team finish as runners-up in the Second Division to return to the top flight. He scored a hat trick in his final appearance with the Hammers in May 1992, before joining Aston Villa.

5. The Hammers paid a club-record transfer fee of £180,000 to West Bromwich Albion for David Cross in December 1977. Like future West Ham defender Stuart Pearce, Cross was nicknamed "Psycho" and soon became a cult hero. He contributed 97 goals in 224 games, including 33 in 1980-81 to help the side win the Second Division title. Cross then scored 19 goals in his first season in the top flight and once notched all of the goals in a 4-0 away win over Tottenham Hotspur. Cross also helped the squad

win the 1979-1980 FA Cup and reach the League Cup final in 1980-81. He also registered a hat trick in European Winners' Cup victory against Castilla before joining Manchester City in 1982.

6. Eighteen-year-old Clyde Best became one of the first black players for the club, and England in 1969, after having arrived from Bermuda two years earlier. Skipper Bobby Moore took him under his wing, and it didn't take long before he became a fan favorite at Upton Park. Best led the team in scoring in 1971-72 with 23 goals and shared the lead with Billy Bonds in 1973-74 with 13. He totaled 58 goals in 221 appearances for the side before leaving to play in America with Tampa Bay. Best later managed the Bermuda national team and was inducted into the country's National Sports Hall of Fame in 2004.

7. The 1959-60 Hammer of the Year Award went to Malcolm Musgrove as he led the side with 20 goals and went on to register 100 of them in 300 games during his time with the club. He arrived in December 1953 as a winger from a junior team in Scotland and helped the club win the 1957-58 Second Division. He joined Leyton Orient in 1962 and also became chairman of the Professional Footballers' Association. Musgrove hung up his boots in 1966 and managed pro soccer clubs in England and America.

8. Trevor Morley arrived in late 1989 from Manchester City and led the team in scoring in three of his first four full seasons. He helped the side earn promotion to the First

Division by finishing as Second Division runners-up in 1990-91. He missed several games the next campaign and the club was relegated in 1992. Morley then notched 22 goals in 1992-93 to help the team back into the top tier by finishing Second Division runners-up again. He didn't score in his first 16 games in 1994-95 and joined Reading in 1995 after spending some time on loan in Norway with Brann. Morley netted 70 goals in 215 appearances and was voted Hammer of the Year for 1993-94.

9. After arriving in February 1971 from Newcastle United for £120,000, Bryan "Pop" Robson scored in his debut and led the side with 28 goals in 1972-73, when he was named Hammer of the Year. He played just one more season before joining Sunderland in July 1974, for a reported £145,000. Robson came back to Upton Park in October 1976 and led the squad in scoring for the next three seasons, before joining hometown team Sunderland in June 1979. Robson scored 104 times in 255 outings for West Ham and entered coaching after giving up playing.

10. English international Johnny Byrne joined the club from Crystal Palace in 1962 for a Second Division transfer record of £65,000. Nicknamed "Budgie" because of his constant talking, he led the team in scoring in 1963-64 with 33 goals and again the next season when he tallied 30. He was also named Hammer of the Year in 1963-64 as the team won the FA Cup. He helped the side reach the 1964-65 European Cup Winners' Cup final but had to sit it out due to injury as his teammates hoisted the trophy and

the side also shared the FA Charity Shield. West Ham reached the 1965-66 League Cup final and Byrne posted 108 goals in 206 games before returning to Crystal Palace in 1967.

CHAPTER 8:

NOTABLE TRANSFERS/SIGNINGS

QUIZ TIME!

1. Who is West Ham's most expensive transfer signing?

    a. Pablo Fornals

    b. Issa Diop

    c. Felipe Anderson

    d. Sébastien Haller

2. The Hammers acquired four players at a transfer fee of over £10 million each in 2019-20.

    a. True

    b. False

3. Who was West Ham's most transfer signing in 2016-17?

    a. Javier Hernández (Chicharito)

    b. Manuel Lanzini

    c. Robert Snodgrass

    d. André Ayew

4. The top transfer fee received by the club was for which player?

a. Marko Arnautović
b. Dimitri Payet
c. Rio Ferdinand
d. Carlos Tevez

5. Which side did West Ham sign Andriy Yarmolenko from?

a. FC Schalke 04
b. Linzer ASK
c. Borussia Dortmund
d. FC Rukh Lviv

6. How much did West Ham pay to acquire Felipe Anderson?

a. £39.75 million
b. £36 million
c. £34.20 million
d. £27 million

7. The Hammers signed Sébastien Haller from French club AJ Auxerre in 2019-20.

a. True
b. False

8. What was the transfer fee the Hammers received for Rio Ferdinand?

a. £23.40 million
b. £19 million
c. £15.50 million
d. £12 million

9. To which team did West Ham transfer Marko Arnautović?

   a. Ajax
   b. Inter Milan
   c. Liverpool FC
   d. Shanghai Port FC

10. Who was the club's most expensive transfer signing in 2001-02?

   a. David James
   b. Tomáš Řepka
   c. Frédéric Kanouté
   d. Don Hutchison

11. How much did West Ham pay to acquire Pablo Fornals?

   a. £33 million
   b. £28 million
   c. £25.20 million
   d. £22.50 million

12. Javier Mascherano played just seven matches with West Ham before being sold to Liverpool FC.

   a. True
   b. False

13. Who was the club's most expensive departure in 2011-12?

   a. Scott Parker
   b. Nicky Maynard
   c. Alessandro Diamanti
   d. Radoslav Kováč

14. Which outfit did the Hammers sell Carlos Tevez to in 2009-10?

    a. Atlético Madrid
    b. Manchester City FC
    c. Juventus
    d. Manchester United

15. What was the transfer fee West Ham received for Dimitri Payet?

    a. £35 million
    b. £31.90 million
    c. £28 million
    d. £26.37 million

16. The Hammers signed 3 players from SC Corinthians in 2006-07.

    a. True
    b. False

17. West Ham sold which player to Middlesbrough FC for £7.11 million in 2015-16?

    a. Mohamed Diamé
    b. James Tomkins
    c. Stewart Downing
    d. Modibo Maïga

18. How much did the Hammers pay to acquire Sébastien Haller?

    a. £34 million
    b. £37 million

c. £40.25 million

d. £45 million

19. From which club did West Ham sign Felipe Anderson?

a. RCD Espanyol

b. AC Milan

c. Paris FC

d. SS Lazio

20. West Ham sold André Ayew to Swansea City FC for £10 million.

a. True

b. False

QUIZ ANSWERS

1. D – Sébastien Haller

2. A – True

3. D – André Ayew

4. B – Dimitri Payet

5. C – Borussia Dortmund

6. C – £34.20 million

7. B – False

8. A – £23.40 million

9. D – Shanghai Port FC

10. B – Tomáš Řepka

11. C – £25.20 million

12. A – True

13. A – Scott Parker

14. B – Manchester City FC

15. D – £26.37 million

16. B – False

17. C – Stewart Downing

18. D – £45 million

19. D – SS Lazio

20. B – False

DID YOU KNOW?

1. The top five transfer fees paid by West Ham are forward Sébastien Haller from Eintracht Frankfurt for £45 million in 2019-20, midfielder Felipe Anderson from SS Lazio for £34.2 million in 2019-20, midfielder Pablo Fornals from Villarreal CF for £25.2 million in 2019-20, defender Issa Diop from FC Toulouse for £22.5 million in 2018-19, and forward André Ayew from Swansea City for £21.69 million in 2016-17.

2. The top five transfer fees received by the club are winger Dimitri Payet to Olympique Marseille for £26.37 million in 2016-17, forward Carlos Tevez to Manchester City for £26.1 million in 2009-10, defender Rio Ferdinand to Leeds United for £23.4 million in 2000-01, forward Marko Arnautović to Shanghai SIPG for £22.5 million in 2019-20, and forward André Ayew to Swansea City for £20.52 million in 2017-18.

3. The club's record arrival so far has been French-born, Ivory Coast international forward Sébastien Haller. He arrived in July 2019 from Eintracht Frankfurt for a fee of £45 million and signed a five-year contract. In July 2020, Frankfurt reported West Ham to FIFA after the English club failed to pay a transfer installment of £5.4 million two months earlier. The Hammers claimed they withheld the payment due to a contract dispute between the two clubs.

Haller scored 14 goals in 54 games before being sold to Dutch club Ajax for £20.25 million for a loss of nearly £25 million.

4. It looks as if West Ham made another questionable signing in their second-most expensive signing by acquiring Brazilian international midfielder Felipe Anderson. They paid the Italian side SS Lazio £34.2 million for him in July 2018, and he scored 10 goals in 40 games in his first season but just 1 goal in 28 outings in his second. Anderson was then loaned to Porto for the 2020-21 campaign after scoring 12 times in 73 appearances with the Hammers.

5. Spanish international midfielder Pablo Fornals joined the club in June 2019 from Villarreal CF for a fee of £25.2 million and then signed a five-year deal. Fornals started his pro career with Malaga and helped Spain win the UEFA European Under-21 Championship in 2019. He notched 7 goals in 63 games with Malaga, 9 goals in 96 outings with Villarreal, and 7 goals in 67 contests with the Hammers as of April 14, 2021.

6. When center-back Issa Diop of France arrived in June 2018 from Toulouse, he was West Ham's most expensive signing at the time at £22.5 million. Unfortunately, he became the first Hammers player to score an own goal in his Premier League debut during a 3-1 away loss to Arsenal. He scored his first goal for his own team three days later in a 3-1 League Cup win over AFC Wimbledon. On Sept. 22, 2020, Diop tested positive for COVID-19 and missed the side's League Cup match with Hull City. On

Feb. 9, 2021, Diop became the first concussion substitute in English soccer in an FA Cup outing against Manchester United when he was replaced by Ryan Fredericks. Currently he has had made 92 appearances for the side.

7. West Ham had success with Austrian international forward Marko Arnautović. He cost £20.07 million from Stoke City in July 2017 and was sold to Shanghai SIPG in China for £22.5 million two years later. In between, he was named Hammer of the Year for 2017-18 after scoring 11 goals in 35 games and was named Austrian Footballer of the Year for 2018. He followed up with another 11 goals in 30 games the next season to lead the side in scoring. Even though Arnautović signed a new contract with West Ham in January 2019, which saw his wages increase by 20 percent, he was soon sold to Shanghai.

8. The winner of the 2015-16 Hammer of the Year Award was French international Dimitri Payet, who was born on the Indian Ocean island of Réunion in East Africa. He arrived in June 2015 from Marseille for a reported £10.7 million fee and signed a five-year contract. He scored 9 league goals and 12 in all competitions in 38 games to impress the fans and management and was named to the PFA Premier League Team of the Year. He inked a new 5½-year contract in February 2016 which reportedly paid him £125,000 a week but his second season was interrupted by injury, and he scored 3 goals in 22 outings. Payet was then sold back to Marseille in January 2017 for a Hammers' record sale of £26.37 million.

9. Ghanaian international forward André Ayew was transferred from Swansea City for £21.69 million in August 2016 but was sold back to Swansea in January 2018 for £20.52 million. He scored 6 goals in 26 games in his first season and chipped in with another 6 in 24 matches before being sent back to Swansea. Ayew was later loaned by Swansea to Fenerbahçe of Turkey for the 2018-19 campaign but was back with the Welsh club the following season. Ayew currently remains with Swansea in and has scored 129 goals in 481 career club games, with 19 goals in 91 outings for Ghana.

10. West Ham's bid of £4 million for English international defender Matthew Upson was turned down by Birmingham City in January 2007. The club upped the bid to a reported £6 million with add-ons, depending on the number of appearances he made. Upson then joined the side and signed a 4½-year contract. He first wore the captain's armband in August 2007 and was given it full-time two years later when former skipper Lucas Neill departed. The Hammers were relegated from the Premier League in May 2011, and after 145 appearances, Upson joined Stoke City.

CHAPTER 9:

ODDS & ENDS

QUIZ TIME!

1. What is the most wins West Ham has recorded in a domestic league season?

   a. 23
   b. 27
   c. 28
   d. 31

2. Andy Malcolm was the first player to win the club's Hammer of the Year Award, back in 1958.

   a. True
   b. False

3. Who was the youngest player to make an appearance for the Hammers, at the age of 16 years and 198 days?

   a. Chris Cohen
   b. Neil Finn
   c. Domingos Quina
   d. Reece Oxford

4. West Ham's biggest Premier League victory was 6-0 against which club?

    a. Derby County FC

    b. Manchester City FC

    c. Sunderland AFC

    d. Barnsley FC

5. What is the fewest games West Ham has won in a domestic league season?

    a. 10

    b. 8

    c. 7

    d. 5

6. Which player scored a club-record 6 goals in one game against Leeds United on February 9, 1929?

    a. Jimmy Ruffell

    b. Vic Watson

    c. Syd Puddefoot

    d. Vivian Gibbins

7. Former Hammers' striker Teddy Sheringham is the oldest goal-scorer in Premier League history, as of 2020.

    a. True

    b. False

8. What is the most points West Ham recorded in a season?

    a. 76

    b. 82

c. 88

d. 91

9. Which player won the Hammer of the Year Award five times?

   a. Julian Dicks

   b. Trevor Brooking

   c. Billy Bonds

   d. Bobby Moore

10. What year was the West Ham United Women's team founded?

    a. 1988

    b. 1991

    c. 1995

    d. 2002

11. Who was the oldest player to make an appearance for West Ham, at the age of 41 years and 226 days.

    a. Teddy Sheringham

    b. Jussi Jääskeläinen

    c. Billy Bonds

    d. Les Sealey

12. West Ham scored 101 goals in the 1957-58 First Division.

    a. True

    b. False

13. The Hammer's biggest victory in any competition was 10-0 against what club in the second round of the 1983 League Cup?

a. Brentford FC

b. Stockport County FC

c. Newcastle United

d. Bury FC

14. The club's biggest defeat was 8-2 to which outfit?

a. Chelsea FC

b. Southampton FC

c. Sheffield Wednesday

d. Blackburn Rovers

15. How many games did West Ham draw in the 1968-69 domestic league season?

a. 10

b. 16

c. 18

d. 21

16. West Ham won the BBC Sports Team of the Year Award in 1965.

a. True

b. False

17. Who won the club's first Young Hammer of the Year Award in 2008?

a. Freddie Sears

b. Zavon Hines

c. Jack Collison

d. James Tomkins

18. The Dockers Derby is the name of the rivalry between West Ham and which club?

    a. Tottenham Hotspur
    b. Millwall FC
    c. Fulham FC
    d. Crystal Palace FC

19. The most losses suffered by the club in a domestic league season is?

    a. 25
    b. 23
    c. 21
    d. 18

20. West Ham played in the first FA Cup final ever hosted at Wembley Stadium.

    a. True
    b. False

QUIZ ANSWERS

1. C – 28

2. A – True

3. D – Reece Oxford

4. D – Barnsley FC

5. C – 7

6. B – Vic Watson

7. A – True

8. C – 88

9. B – Trevor Brooking

10. B – 1991

11. C – Billy Bonds

12. A – True

13. D – Bury FC

14. D – Blackburn Rovers

15. C – 18

16. A – True

17. D – James Tomkins

18. B – Millwall FC

19. B – 23

20. A – True

DID YOU KNOW?

1. Arnold Hills, the owner of Thames Ironworks, was a talented soccer player who represented Oxford against Cambridge in the varsity match. He was also a university track and field champion and played for Oxford University in the 1876-77 FA Cup final in a 2-1 defeat to Wanderers FC after extra time. Hills played with the Old Harrovians for several seasons and in 1879 played for England against Scotland in a 5-4 English victory.

2. The Hammers have played at five different home venues since being formed. The club's first home ground was Hermit Road in Canning Town in 1895 before moving to Browning Road in East Ham in March 1897. The side then moved to the Memorial Grounds in the summer of 1897 and to the Boleyn Ground in Upton Park in 1904. In 2016, the side moved to London Stadium.

3. The club's biggest crowds have been at London Stadium. Its record league attendance was 59,988 vs Everton, in a Premier League match on March 30, 2019. The record FA Cup attendance was 56,975 vs Manchester City in the third round on January 6, 2017, and the biggest League Cup crowd was 50,270 vs Tottenham Hotspur, in the fourth round on October 31, 2018.

4. London Stadium was originally named Olympic Stadium and then Stadium at Queen Elizabeth Olympic Park. It's a

multi-purpose outdoor facility located at Queen Elizabeth Olympic Park in the Stratford area of London. The venue was built for the 2012 Summer Olympics and Paralympics, for track and field events, as well as the opening and closing ceremonies. It held 80,000 for the Olympics but re-opened in July 2016 with a capacity of 66,000. However, the capacity for soccer games is limited to 60,000.

5. West Ham supporters are famous for singing the chorus of their team's anthem, "I'm Forever Blowing Bubbles." The song was first introduced to the club in the late 1920s by manager Charlie Paynter and it is always played before home games with the crowd joining in. When the players come onto the pitch, they're met with thousands of bubbles which are created by machines at the stadium. Since the 1950s fans have also sung the East London pub song named "Knees Up, Mother Brown."

6. Unfortunately, the club was associated with soccer hooliganism in the past. The 1989 movie *The Firm*, which starred Gary Oldman, was based on organized West Ham hooligan gangs as was the 2005 movie *Green Street Hooligans*, which starred Elijah Wood and Charlie Hunnam. Several other movies deal with the topic such as *Inter City Firm*, *Green Street 2: Stand Your Ground*, *Green Street 3: Never Back Down*, and *Cass*."

7. West Ham has natural geographical rivalries with other London-based clubs, such as Tottenham Hotspur, Chelsea, Arsenal, Crystal Palace Fulham, and Queens Park Rangers.

The club also has a rivalry with Sheffield United. However, the fiercest and oldest rivalry is with Millwall because the early history of the clubs is intertwined. Sadly, a Millwall supporter died at New Cross station in 1972 after falling out of a train during a fight with Hammers' supporters and there have been numerous other instances of violence between fans of the two clubs.

8. The club introduced a new annual award in 2013 known as the West Ham United Lifetime Achievement Award. Those who have had the honor of receiving it as of April 2021 are: 2013 Billy Bonds, 2014 Trevor Brooking, 2015 Martin Peters, 2016 Geoff Hurst, 2017 Bobby Moore, 2018 Ken Brown, and 2019 Ronnie Boyce.

9. The youngest West Ham player was Reece Oxford, who competed at the age of 16 years and 198 days, when he took to the pitch against FC Lusitanos at home in a Europa League first qualifying round game on July 2, 2015. The oldest player was Billy Bonds at 41 years and 226 days against Southampton in a First Division contest on April 20, 1988.

10. West Ham United Women Football Club was originally formed in 1991 and plays its home games at Dagenham & Redbridge's Chigwell Construction Stadium on Victoria Road, which has a capacity of just over 6,000. The side currently plays in the Football Association Women's Super League (FA WSL), which is the top tier for women's soccer in England. In July 2018 the West Ham Ladies changed their name to West Ham United Women's Team.

CHAPTER 10:

DOMESTIC COMPETITION

QUIZ TIME!

1. How many times did West Ham win the London Challenge Cup?

   a. 3
   b. 7
   c. 9
   d. 12

2. West Ham has never won a top-tier championship or League Cup.

   a. True
   b. False

3. Which season did the Hammers reach their first FA Cup final?

   a. 1919-20
   b. 1922-23
   c. 1947-48
   d. 1960-61

4. What was the first honor the club won?

    a. Southern League Second Division
    b. West Ham Charity Cup
    c. London League
    d. London Charity Cup

5. How many times has West Ham won the second-tier Second Division/Championship League, as of 2020?

    a. 2
    b. 0
    c. 5
    d. 3

6. Which side did West Ham play in its first FA Cup final?

    a. Derby County FC
    b. Charlton Athletic
    c. Bolton Wanderers
    d. Sheffield United

7. The Hammers have played in six FA Charity/Community Shield games.

    a. True
    b. False

8. West Ham played which club in the 1980-81 League Cup final?

    a. Manchester City FC
    b. Liverpool FC
    c. Coventry City Fc
    d. Watford FC

9. How many points did West Ham record to win its first Second Division championship?

   a. 51
   b. 44
   c. 62
   d. 57

10. Who scored the winning goal in the 1963-64 FA Cup final?

    a. Ronnie Boyce
    b. Geoff Hurst
    c. Johnny Byrne
    d. John Sissons

11. Which club did the Hammers defeat to win the 1963-64 FA Cup?

    a. Swansea City FC
    b. Preston North End
    c. Oxford United
    d. Manchester United

12. West Ham shared the 1964 FA Charity Shield honors with Everton FC.

    a. True
    b. False

13. Which year were the Hammers champions of the Western League?

    a. 1903
    b. 1905

c. 1907

d. 1910

14. The Hammers met which outfit in the 1965-66 League Cup final?

   a. Grimsby Town FC

   b. Cardiff City FC

   c. Peterborough United

   d. West Bromwich Albion

15. How many times has West Ham reached the FA Cup final?

   a. 3

   b. 5

   c. 6

   d. 8

16. The Hammers were outright winners of the 1980 FA Charity Shield.

   a. True

   b. False

17. Which team did West Ham beat to win the 1979-80 FA Cup?

   a. Arsenal FC

   b. Liverpool FC

   c. Tottenham Hotspur

   d. Leeds United

18. How many times has West Ham been runners-up in the second-tier Second Division/Championship League?

a. a. 1
b. 3
c. 5
d. 7

19. Who scored the winning goal in the 1979-80 FA Cup final?

    a. Stuart Pearson
    b. David Cross
    c. Paul Allen
    d. Trevor Brooking

20. The Hammers were the first winners of the Football League War Cup.

    a. True
    b. False

QUIZ ANSWERS

1. C – 9

2. A – True

3. B – 1922-23

4. B – West Ham Charity Cup

5. A – 2

6. C – Bolton Wanderers

7. B – False

8. B – Liverpool FC

9. D – 57

10. A – Ronnie Boyce

11. B – Preston North End

12. B – False

13. C – 1907

14. D – West Bromwich Albion

15. C – 5

16. B - False

17. A – Arsenal FC

18. B – 3

19. D – Trevor Brooking

20. A – True

DID YOU KNOW?

1. The Hammers have yet to hoist a top-tier English League championship or a League Cup. However, the club has won two second-tier titles and two second-tier playoffs. They have also captured three FA Cups and shared an FA Charity Shield.

2. The squad has been relegated in English Football League action on six occasions. They fell from the First to Second Division following the 1931-32, 1977-78, 1988-89, and 1991-92 seasons. The club was also relegated from the Premier League to the second-tier Division One after the 2002-03 campaign and from the Premier League to the second-tier Championship League after the 2020-21 season.

3. The Hammers won the second-tier Second Division in 1957-58 and 1980-81 and were runners-up in 1922-23, 1990-91, and 1992-93. They won the second-tier Championship League playoffs in 2004-05 and 2011-12 to earn promotion back to the Premier League.

4. The team's FA Cup championships took place in 1963-64 with a 3-2 victory over Preston North End, in 1974-75 when they beat Fulham 2-0, and in 1979-80 when they edged Arsenal 1-0. They were runners-up in 1922-23 when they were downed 2-0 by Bolton Wanderers and again in 2005-06 when they drew Liverpool 3-3 but were then beaten 3-1 in the deciding penalty shootout.

5. The Hammers reached the League Cup final in 1965-66 which was the last season the competition was decided over two legs. They were downed 5-3 on aggregate by West Bromwich Albion after winning the first leg 2-1 at home but losing the second leg 4-1 away. They returned to the final in 1980-81 and drew Liverpool 0-0 in front of 100,000 fans at Wembley Stadium. The game went to extra time with Liverpool taking the lead two minutes from time and West Ham equalizing in the final minute. The match was replayed two weeks later with 36,693 fans in attendance at Villa Park in Birmingham. Liverpool won 2-1.

6. The Hammers shared the 1964 FA Charity Shield by drawing Liverpool 2-2 at Anfield in Liverpool. They were runners-up in 1975 when they lost 2-0 to Derby County at Wembley and met Liverpool again in 1980, this time at Wembley, and were edged 1-0.

7. Before joining the English Football League in 1919-20, the Hammers were crowned champions and Section A Champions of the Western League in 1906-07. During World War II, the FA Cup was put on hold and replaced by the Football League War Cup. West Ham won the 1939-40 title by beating Blackburn Rovers 1-0.

8. The club has also won several minor English titles over the years as well as finishing as runners-up in competitions such as the Southern Floodlit Cup, the London Challenge Cup, the Essex Professional Cup, and the London Charity

Cup. The club's youth squad won the FA Youth Cup in 1962-1963, 1980-81, and 1998-99 and finished as runners-up in 1956-57, 1958-59, 1974-75, and 1995-96.

9. While the club competed as Thames Ironworks FC until changing its name to West Ham United in 1900, it was crowned winners of the West Ham Charity Cup in 1896 and runners-up in 1897, London League champions in 1897-98 and runners-up in 1896-97, champions of the Southern League Division Two in 1898-99, and London Champions in 1898-99.

10. The club's biggest home Premier League win was 6-0 at home vs Barnsley in 1998, and 5-0 away vs Derby County in 2007. The biggest First Division triumphs were 8-0 at home vs Sunderland in 1968, and 6-1 away over Manchester City in 1962. Their record FA Cup wins were 8-1 at home vs Chesterfield in January 1914, and 5-0 away vs Chatham in 1903. The biggest League Cup victories were 10-0 vs Bury at home in 1983, and 5-1 away over Cardiff City in 1996, and 5-1 away over Walsall in 1967.

CHAPTER 11:

EUROPE AND BEYOND

QUIZ TIME!

1. What was the first international tournament West Ham participated in?

    a. Anglo-Italian League Cup
    b. International Soccer League
    c. European Cup Winners' Cup
    d. EUFA Europa League

2. The Hammers have never participated in the UEFA Champions League.

    a. True
    b. False

3. What was the first club West Ham played in a UEFA tournament?

    a. FC Lausanne-Sport
    b. Real Zaragoza
    c. AC Sparta Prague
    d. K.A.A. Gent

4. How many times did the Hammers participate in the UEFA Cup Winners' Cup?

    a. 6

    b. 4

    c. 3

    d. 1

5. Which year did West Ham win the UEFA Intertoto Cup?

    a. 2005

    b. 2002

    c. 1999

    d. 1995

6. The Hammers faced which team in the 1975 Anglo-Italian League Cup?

    a. AS Roma

    b. S.S.C. Napoli

    c. Bologna FC

    d. ACF Fiorentina

7. Johnny Byrne is West Ham's top scorer in UEFA competitions with 8 goals.

    a. True

    b. False

8. How many games has West Ham played in UEFA competitions?

    a. 45

    b. 52

c. 58

d. 62

9. Which club did the Hammers defeat to win the 1964-65 European Cup Winners' Cup?

    a. GNK Dinamo Zagreb

    b. Real Zaragoza

    c. TSV 1860 Munich

    d. Torino FC

10. Who scored the winning goal in the second leg of the 1999 Intertoto Cup final?

    a. Steve Potts

    b. Trevor Sinclair

    c. Paulo Wanchope

    d. Frank Lampard Sr.

11. Which team eliminated the Hammers in the 2016-17 UEFA Europa League?

    a. SK Rapid Wien

    b. Grasshopper Club Zürich

    c. NK Domžale

    d. FC Astra Giurgiu

12. The Hammers lost the 1975-76 European Cup Winners' Cup in a penalty shootout.

    a. True

    b. False

13. Who scored the winning goal in the 1964-65 European Cup Winners' Cup final?

a. Brian Dear

b. Alan Sealey

c. John Sissons

d. Geoff Hurst

14. How many games has West Ham won in all UEFA tournaments?

    a. 25

    b. 36

    c. 23

    d. 40

15. Which round did West Ham reach in the 1999-00 UEFA Cup?

    a. Semi-finals

    b. Quarterfinals

    c. Second Round

    d. First Round

16. The Hammers have appeared in three UEFA Cup/Europa League tournaments.

    a. True

    b. False

17. West Ham faced which side in the 1975-76 European Cup Winners' Cup final?

    a. ADO Den Haag

    b. Wrexham AFC

    c. Eintracht Frankfurt

    d. R.S.C. Anderlecht

18. Which round of the 1965-66 European Cup Winners' Cup did the Hammers reach?

    a. Second round
    b. Quarterfinals
    c. Semi-finals
    d. Finals

19. West Ham defeated which squad in the 1999 Intertoto Cup final?

    a. FC Jokerit
    b. Juventus
    c. FC Metz
    d. SC Heerenveen

20. The Hammers have scored over 80 goals in UEFA competitions.

    a. True
    b. False

QUIZ ANSWERS

1. B – European Cup Winners' Cup

2. A – True

3. D – K.A.A. Gent

4. C – 3

5. C – 1999

6. D – ACF Fiorentina

7. B – False

8. B – 52

9. C – TSV 1860 Munich

10. C – Paulo Wanchope

11. D – FC Astra Giurgiu

12. B – False

13. B – Alan Sealey

14. A – 25

15. C – Second Round

16. A – True

17. D – R.S.C. Anderlecht

18. C – Semi-finals

19. C – FC Metz

20. A – True

DID YOU KNOW?

1. West Ham has competed in UEFA tournaments nine times, in two different non-UEFA competitions. The club's first venture into Europe came in 1964-65 in the European Cup Winners' Cup and the latest trip was in 2016-17 when the Hammers played in the Europa League. Their lone victory in UEFA events so far was capturing the European Cup Winners' Cup in 1964-65.

2. The Hammers won the 1964-65 European Cup Winners' Cup by beating 1860 Munich 2-0 in front of nearly 100,000 fans at Wembley Stadium on May 19, 1965. They had qualified by winning the previous campaign's FA Cup. Alan Sealey was the hero with goals in the 70th and 72nd minutes, and goalkeeper Jim Standen earned the clean sheet. West Ham beat Gent of Belgium 2-1 on aggregate in the first round, Spartak Praha Sokolovo of the Czech Republic 3-2 on aggregate in the second round, Lausanne-Sport of Switzerland 6-4 on aggregate in the quarterfinals, and Real Zaragoza of Spain 3-2 on aggregate in the semi-finals.

3. As reigning champions, the Hammers received a buy-in the first round of the 1965-66 European Cup Winners' Cup. They beat Greek side Olympiacos 6-2 on aggregate in the second round, with a 4-0 home win in the first leg followed by a 2-2 away draw in the second leg. They then

disposed of 1. FC Magdeburg of East Germany 2-1 on aggregate in the quarterfinals with a 1-0 home win and a 1-1 away draw. They then met Borussia Dortmund of West Germany in the semi-finals. Dortmund won the first leg 2-1 at Upton Park, scoring 2 goals in the last four minutes of the game to overcome a 1-0 deficit. The German side followed up with a 3-1 home victory in the second leg to win 5-2 on aggregate.

4. A decade passed before the Hammers reached the European Cup Winners' Cup tournament again, in 1975-76. They handled Lahden Reipas of Finland 5-2 on aggregate in the first round and doubled Ararat Erevan of Armenia 4-2 on aggregate in the second round. They faced Dutch side FC Den Haag in the quarterfinals and advanced via the away-goals rule after drawing 5-5 on aggregate. The Hammers edged Eintracht Frankfurt 4-3 on aggregate in the semi-finals and met Anderlecht of Belgium in the final. However, after taking a lead in the 28th minute, they were beaten 4-2.

5. After winning the 1979-80 FA Cup, West Ham qualified for the Cup Winners' Cup again in 1980-81 while playing in the English second-tier Second Division. Crowd violence broke out at the Bernabéu Stadium in Spain during the first-leg 3-1 loss to Castilla and a West Ham supporter lost his life. The Hammers were forced to play the return leg at home, behind closed doors, and won 5-1 to advance 6-4 on aggregate. They met Romanian side Poli Timișoara in the second leg and won 4-1 on aggregate

before losing to eventual cup winners Dynamo Tbilisi of Georgia 4-2 on aggregate in the quarterfinals.

6. In 1999, West Ham qualified for the Intertoto Cup after finishing in fifth place in the Premier League the previous season and received a bye for the first two rounds. The Hammers met Finnish side Jokerit in the third round and won 2-1 on aggregate. The squad beat Dutch side Heerenveen 2-0 on aggregate in the semi-finals to reach the final against Metz of France. They were edged 1-0 at home in the first leg but bounced back to win 3-1 away to hoist the trophy. This enabled them to qualify for the 1999-200 UEFA Cup as one of the three Intertoto Cup winners that season.

7. In the 1999-2000 UEFA Cup, West Ham beat Croatian side Osijek 3-0 at home in the first leg and 3-1 away in the second leg to advance 6-1 on aggregate. In the second round, the Hammers faced Romanian team Steaua București, and lost the first leg away 2-0 while drawing 0-0 at Upton Park in the second leg, to lose 2-0 on aggregate. The club qualified for the UEFA Cup for just the second time in 2006-07 by finishing as runners-up in the 2005-06 FA Cup. There were violent scenes in Italy before and after their 3-0 loss to Palermo in the first leg and they were beaten 1-0 at home in the second leg to lose 4-0 on aggregate.

8. West Ham's first trip to the Europa League, formerly the UEFA Cup, came in 2015-16 after the team qualified by

winning the Premier League Fair Play table the previous season. They entered the competition at the first qualifying round and beat Lusitanos of Andorra 4-0 on aggregate. In the 3-0 first-leg home win, 16-year-old Reece Oxford made his debut to become West Ham's youngest player. In the second qualifying round, the Hammers drew 1-1 on aggregate against Maltese side Birkirkara. They played 30 minutes of extra time and West Ham advanced 5-3 in the penalty shootout. The club made its exit in the third qualifying round, losing 4-3 on aggregate to Romanian club Astra Giurgiu.

9. The seventh-place Hammers qualified for the 2016-17 Europa League after FA Cup winners Manchester United had already qualified and their cup winners' spot went to West Ham. The team met Domžale of Slovenia in the third qualifying round and won 4-1 on aggregate. In the playoff round, the Hammers fell 2-1 on aggregate to Romanian Liga I champions Astra Giurgiu and were eliminated by the team for the second straight year in the competition.

10. In non-UEFA European tournaments, West Ham participated in the Anglo-Italian League Cup in 1975. This was an event between the FA Cup winners and the winners of the Coppa Italia in Italy. The Hammers met Fiorentina and were beaten 1-0 in both legs to lose 2-0 on aggregate. In 1992-93, the Hammers played in the Anglo-Italian Cup, which featured four Italian and four English teams. West Ham played each Italian side once. They lost 2-0 away to Cremonese, beat Reggiana 2-0 at home, beat

Cosenza 1-0 away, and drew 0-0 at home with Pisa. They finished in third place in the English section of the group and were eliminated.

CHAPTER 12:

TOP SCORERS

QUIZ TIME!

1. Who has scored the most goals in all competitions for the club?

    a. Geoff Hurst

    b. John Dick

    c. Vic Watson

    d. Syd Puddefoot

2. George Ratcliffe was the first player to lead West Ham in scoring in the Southern League.

    a. True

    b. False

3. How many goals did Carlton Cole lead the Hammers with in the 2011-12 Championship League?

    a. 7

    b. 9

    c. 12

    d. 14

4. Who led the squad in scoring in the 1993-94 Premier League?

   a. Matt Holland
   b. Lee Chapman
   c. Steve Jones
   d. Trevor Morley

5. How many different players have won a Golden Boot award for West Ham?

   a. 2
   b. 3
   c. 5
   d. 7

6. Who led the Hammers in the 2004-05 domestic league with 20 goals?

   a. Mark Noble
   b. Teddy Sheringham
   c. Marlon Harewood
   d. Youssef Sofiane

7. Vic Watson once scored 50 goals in a season in all competitions for the club.

   a. True
   b. False

8. How many goals did John Dick score in all competitions with West Ham?

   a. 128
   b. 219

c. 166

d. 185

9. These two players led the club in scoring with 9 goals each in the 2015-16 domestic league.

    a. Michail Antonio and Mark Noble

    b. Dimitri Payet and Andy Carroll

    c. Manuel Lanzini and Enner Valencia

    d. Cheikhou Kouyaté and Diafra Sakho

10. How many league goals did Vic Watson tally in 1929-30?

    a. 50

    b. 42

    c. 38

    d. 26

11. Which player led the team with 16 goals in the 1999-2000 Premier League?

    a. Michael Carrick

    b. Steve Lomas

    c. Paul Kitson

    d. Paolo Di Canio

12. Geoff Hurst led the side in scoring in all competitions for six consecutive seasons, from 1965-66 through 1970-71.

    a. True

    b. False

13. How many goals did Jimmy Ruffell score in all competitions with the Hammers?

a. 166

b. 183

c. 210

d. 230

14. Which player won a 1972-73 Golden Boot award with 28 goals?

    a. Alan Taylor

    b. Bryan "Pop" Robson

    c. David Cross

    d. Clyde Best

15. Who led West Ham with 10 goals in the 2019-20 Premier League?

    a. Javier Hernández

    b. Marko Arnautović

    c. Felipe Anderson

    d. Michail Antonio

16. West Ham had three different players lead the club in domestic league scoring with 9 goals each in 2006-07.

    a. True

    b. False

17. How many goals did Geoff Hurst net in all competitions?

    a. 311

    b. 284

    c. 249

    d. 230

18. Who led the club with 15 goals in the 1997-98 domestic league?

    a. John Hartson

    b. Julian Dicks

    c. Tony Cottee

    d. Ian Wright

19. How many goals did Vic Watson notch in all competitions with the Hammers?

    a. 221

    b. 253

    c. 297

    d. 326

20. Terry Woodgate set the club record for most goals in a season in all competitions with 54 in 1950-51.

    a. True

    b. False

QUIZ ANSWERS

1. C – Vic Watson

2. B – False

3. D – 14

4. D – Trevor Morley

5. A – 2

6. B – Teddy Sheringham

7. A – True

8. C – 166

9. B – Dimitri Payet and Andy Carroll

10. B – 42

11. D – Paolo Di Canio

12. A – True

13. A – 166

14. B – Bryan "Pop" Robson

15. D – Michail Antonio

16. B – False

17. C – 249

18. A – John Hartson

19. D – 326

20. B – False

DID YOU KNOW?

1. The top 15 scorers in club history when it comes to official non-wartime goals in the English Football League are: Vic Watson 326, Geoff Hurst 249, John Dick 166, Jimmy Ruffell 166, Tony Cottee 146, Johnny Byrne 107, Bryan "Pop" Robson 104, Trevor Brooking 102, Malcolm Musgrove 100, Martin Peters 100, David Cross 97, Ray Stewart 84, Syd Puddefoot 72, Trevor Morley 70, and Paul Goddard 69. All players hail from England except John Dick and Ray Stewart, both of whom were born in Scotland.

2. The most total English Football League goals scored by West Ham players are Vic Watson 298 (1920-1935), Geoff Hurst 180 (1960-1972), Jimmy Ruffell 159 (1921-1937), John Dick 153 (1953-1962), and Tony Cottee 115 (1983-88 and 1994-96).

3. Currently, the most FA Cup goals scored by West Ham players are Vic Watson 28 (1922-1934), Geoff Hurst 23 (1962-1972), Syd Puddefoot 12 (1914-1922), Tony Cottee 12 (1983-1996), and John Dick 11 (1954-1962).

4. The most club goals scored in all competitions in a single season are: Vic Watson 50 (1929-30), Geoff Hurst 41 (1966-67), Geoff Hurst 40 (1965-66), Vic Watson 37 (1926-27), Johnny Byrne 33 (1963-64), and David Cross 33 (1980-81).

5. The most goals scored in a single English Football League season are Vic Watson 42 (1929-30), Vic Watson 34 (1926-

27), Syd Puddefoot 29 (1920-21), Vic Watson 29 (1928-29), and Geoff Hurst 29 (1966-67). The most goals in a single match are: Vic Watson, 6 vs Leeds United at home in the First Division in February 1929, Geoff Hurst, 6 vs Sunderland at home in the First Division in October 1968, and Brian Dear, 5 vs West Bromwich Albion at home in the First Division in April 1965.

6. English international striker Tony Cottee enjoyed two spells with the Hammers and tallied 146 goals in 336 outings to currently rank as the club's fifth all-time leading scorer. He made his debut as a 17-year-old on New Year's Day 1983 and scored. Cottee had notched 37 league goals by the time he turned 20 years old, and was named the PFA Young Player of the Year and Hammer of the Year for 1985-86, when he added another 20 goals. He joined Everton in August 1988 for a £2.2 million fee to set a new British record at the time. Cottee returned to Upton Park in September 1994 and remained until joining Selangor of Malaysia on a free transfer in October 1996.

7. Winger Jimmy Ruffell was signed by West Ham in March 1920 and made his debut the next year. He played 548 times with the club and netted 166 goals while leading the squad in scoring in 1927-28 and 1934-35. He helped the Hammers reach the FA Cup final for the first time in 1922-23, they also earned promotion to the top tier by winning the Second Division. The English international then joined Aldershot briefly in 1937 before hanging up his boots.

Ruffell's brother Bill was also a pro soccer player who was once on the books at West Ham.

8. Scottish forward John Dick was a prolific scorer for West Ham after arriving in 1953 from semi-pro outfit Crittall Athletic. He played 351 matches and contributed 166 goals, before joining Brentford in 1962, for what was then a club-record £17,500 fee. He helped the Hammers capture the Second Division crown in 1957-58 by scoring 21 league goals and 26 in all competitions. He then notched a career-high 27 league goals in the First Division the next season and 30 in all. Dick became the West Ham's first Scottish international in 1959 but played just once for his homeland. He later returned to Upton Park to manage the junior team.

9. Geoff Hurst became an instant hero in 1966 when he became the first man to score a hat trick in a World Cup final as England doubled West Germany 4-2. He made his Hammers' debut as a teenager in 1960 and went on to net 249 goals in 502 appearances. Hurst helped the side win the 1963-64 FA Cup and 1964-65 European Cup Winners' Cup while sharing the 1964 Charity Shield and winning a 1965-66 League Cup runners-up medal. He was voted Hammer of the Year three times and received the West Ham United Lifetime Achievement Award in 2016. He left for Stoke City in 1972 and later managed Chelsea and a club in Kuwait. Hurst, who's in the English Football Hall of Fame, was also an accomplished cricket player.

10. The current all-time leading scorer for the Hammers is Vic Watson with 326 goals in 505 appearances between 1920 and 1935. He arrived from Wellingborough Town and chipped in with 13 hat tricks at West Ham. That included 6 goals in an outing against Leeds in February 1929 and scoring 4 goals in a game on three occasions. He helped the team finish as Second Division runners-up in 1922-23 and they reached the FA Cup final the same season. He then joined Southampton. Watson also tallied 4 goals in five contests for England.

CONCLUSION

The West Ham United story began well over 100 years ago and continues to be written with each passing year. You've just read the comprehensive history of the club in entertaining and educational trivia form from the beginnings in 1895, right up to the 2020-21 English Premier League campaign.

We hope you've enjoyed accompanying us on this amazing journey back through time, and hope you've been entertained along the way, and perhaps have learned something new at the same time.

We've included as many players and managers as possible, and provided a collection of educational facts and trivia regarding the club's records, successes, transfers, etc. However, we apologize if some of your favorite players and managers are missing from our pages, including every member was impossible.

Packed with 12 unique quiz-filled chapters and an array of descriptive "Did You Know" facts, this book should have put you in a prime position to challenge fellow West Ham and soccer fans to an assortment of fun-filled quiz contests. This is the ideal way to determine once and for all who the top dog is when it comes to the club's history.

We hope you'll feel inclined to share this West Ham trivia and fact book with other fans to help spread the word concerning this historic club.

Thank you kindly for being a loyal and passionate Hammers' fan and taking the time and effort to support the club and relive the memories by reading this trivia book.

Printed in Great Britain
by Amazon

35721607R00076